AppleWorks
Word Processing

Books by Arthur Luehrmann and Herbert Peckham
published by the Computer Literacy Press:

AppleWorks Word Processing
A Hands-On Guide

AppleWorks Data Bases
A Hands-On Guide

AppleWorks Spreadsheets
A Hands-On Guide

Hands-On AppleWorks
A Guide to Word Processing,
Data Bases, and Spreadsheets

AppleWorks Word Processing

A Hands-On Guide

Arthur Luehrmann
Herbert Peckham

Computer
Literacy
Press

Gilroy, California

Library of Congress Cataloging-in-Publication Data

Luehrmann, Arthur.
    AppleWorks word processing: a hands-on guide.

    (A computer literacy book)
    Includes index.
    Summary: A hands-on manual, primarily for school use, on how to use the word processing program of a software package called AppleWorks.
    1. AppleWorks (Computer program) 2. Word processing. [1. AppleWorks (Computer program) 2. Word processing] I. Peckham, Herbert D. II. Title. III. Series.
    Z52.5.A68L83   1987   652'.5   87–836
    ISBN 0–941681–01–7

Cover and interior design: Paul Quin
Production coordination: Zipporah W. Collins
Copyediting and technical checking: Loralee Windsor
Typesetting: Computer Literacy Press

Computer tools were used throughout the production of this book. Original writing and editing were done on a personal computer with word processor software similar to that found in AppleWorks. Another computer program converted word processor format commands to typesetting commands in a software system called JustText™. The book design was implemented in the PostScript™ page description language. All art was created directly in PostScript. The final PostScript files were proofed initially on an Apple LaserWriter™ Plus printer. The same files were then typeset on a Linotronic™ 300 compositor. Fonts used are Helvetica®, Times®, ITC Zapf Chancery®, ITC Zapf Dingbats®, and a specially designed proprietary font called AppleDot. The AppleDot font, used mainly in the screen figures, was created with a computer program called Fontographer™.

Computer Literacy Press
353 East Tenth Street, Suite C-624
Gilroy, California   95021-2373

Printed in the United States of America
10 9 8 7 6 5 4   891098

Contents

■ About This Book

Preface for the Teacher

No single application of the computer is as pervasive as word processing. The reason is simple: Nearly everyone writes. Even poor typists and computer novices quickly discover payoffs that come from using word processor software. They find that they are not bothered by concerns about appearance when trying to get their thoughts down, and they see how easy it is to make changes and improvements before printing a final copy of their work.

AppleWorks Word Processing is a hands-on workbook intended to guide students step by step through their first experience in using a word processor software package. The workbook, which assumes no prior computer skills or knowledge on the part of the student, is carefully designed to deal with the many questions, problems, and possible misunderstandings that can arise when the student is working at the computer.

The workbook can be used in a variety of ways. It can serve as a self-study tool for individual students or as a class textbook. It can be used for a unit on word processing in a computer literacy or business education class or as part of the writing and language arts program. The workbook may be especially useful as a supplement to standard computer literacy textbooks that provide little or no hands-on word processor activities.

No special computer expertise is expected of the teacher. Most of the learning takes place while the student is carrying out the computer activities prescribed in the workbook. The teacher's main role, therefore, will not be to present information but to review the computer work with the class and help students gain a better understanding of what they have done.

Workbook Organization

AppleWorks Word Processing is divided into three chapters. Chapter 1 introduces the "survival skills" that students need for all their computer work in the remainder of this book and beyond. Chapter 2 covers the basic word processor tools for entering and editing text. Chapter 3 deals with formatting text for printing.

Chapter 1 Certain features of the software are common to all three applications contained in the Apple-Works package: word processing, working with data bases, and working with spreadsheets. These features are covered in Chapter 1. Students learn to start the computer with the AppleWorks disks, select and give menu commands, create a new file, save a file on a disk, load a file from disk into memory, remove a file from a disk, and leave AppleWorks in an orderly way. The students will continue doing these things throughout the book. These skills also provide a good foundation for future work with data bases and spreadsheets.

Chapter 2 Word processor use has two main aspects. The user is either entering and editing text or specifying the appearance of the text when it is printed. Chapter 2 focuses entirely on the first of these. Students learn the fundamental editing tools: entering, deleting, and inserting text. At first they do these things in a small way, inserting a few characters, deleting a phrase. Later they learn to delete whole blocks of text and to move blocks from one place to another, both within and between files. At the end of the chapter students apply what they have learned in a substantial writing project.

Chapter 3 Formatting is quite different from editing. Editing deals with the content of a document; formatting, the topic of Chapter 3, deals with the document's appearance when it is printed. Students learn how to control page layout, center and justify text, specify headers and footers, and control the type style. They then apply these tools to the writing projects begun in Chapter 2.

It is no accident that *AppleWorks Word Processing* separates the editing tools from the formatting tools. Expert opinion on the teaching of writing emphasizes the need to concentrate on content in the early stages of the writing process without being overly concerned about appearance. Word processor software is especially attractive to teachers of writing because it encourages this separation. Students can enter text, fix mistakes easily, and make revisions long before committing their work to print.

Instructional Design

The overall instructional design of *AppleWorks Word Processing* is based on the common wisdom that experience is the best teacher. Skills learned by doing are far more secure than those learned only by reading.

Classroom setting The material in this workbook is designed for school use. Each chapter is divided into sections called labs. The material in each lab guides students through a sequence of carefully planned activities at the computer. Little or no instructional supervision is required for these labs, which are planned to be completed in one class period.

Software-specific approach Because it is impossible to learn word-processing skills without using some particular word processor software on a computer, good learning materials must come to grips with a myriad of details. This workbook, which assumes that students will use AppleWorks, presents all the specific information needed for their work at the computer.

Curriculum-based approach A major goal of the workbook is that students see the computer as a tool for use throughout the school curriculum. In particular, students should see the obvious benefits of applying word-processing skills to the task of writing. To this end each student undertakes a significant writing project at the end of Chapter 2. Students are led through a sequence of prewriting, writing, and revising activities, as recommended, for example, in the *Handbook for Planning an Effective Writing Program* published by the California State Department of Education.

Relevant examples While learning about word processing, students interact with many text examples. These examples were chosen to serve both the goals of the language arts curriculum and the interests of the students. Examples include the first chapter of Dickens's *A Tale of Two Cities*, a poem by Byron, and, just for fun, a collection of knock-knock jokes. Another set of examples contains errors in punctuation, capitalization, and style for students to edit. Students also learn how to format a standard business letter.

Learning goals Each of the 13 labs begins with a concise list of learning objectives to be accomplished. The overwhelming majority of these are performance objectives: skills that students are expected to acquire as a result of their work at the computer. Along the way, students also learn computer concepts and terminology.

Hands-on approach The backbone of each lab is a sequence of hands-on activities to be carried out at the computer. The physical design of the workbook emphasizes these activities. Directions to the student are printed in a distinctive boldface type to make them stand out from the rest of the text. This makes it easy for students to read instructions, carry them out on the computer, and return to the proper place in the workbook.

Quick-check questions After several hands-on tasks are presented, the workbook provides a few quick-check questions that ask the student, "Do you really understand what you just did?" These quick-check questions reinforce ideas just after they have been experienced and prevent students from simply following directions without paying attention to the results.

Short reviews A brief review or explanation is included from time to time during most labs. Students are expected to turn away from the computer briefly and read these parts for understanding. Like the quick-check questions, these reviews develop additional insight and a deeper understanding of what is going on. The reviews are useful for classroom discussion of the lab activities.

On Your Own activities Nearly all the labs have activities at the end for students who finish early. These "On Your Own" activities are intended to allow students to practice what they have learned, explore on their own, and reinforce their understanding. In contrast to the directed hands-on activities in each lab, the open-ended On Your Own activities give only general guidelines. The main instructional purpose of these activities is to give the students confidence that they can, without detailed guidance, use the tools introduced in the lab.

Review questions The final component of each lab is a set of review questions covering all the material presented. This is yet another opportunity to make certain that students understand what they have done and read. The questions may be answered while in the lab, as seat work in the classroom, or as homework.

Chapter glossaries A glossary appears at the end of each chapter. Included in each glossary are the new AppleWorks commands and vocabulary introduced in the chapter. The vocabulary terms also appear in boldface type when they first appear in the chapter. (The glossary in the accompanying Teacher's Guide is a compilation of the three chapter glossaries in the workbook.)

Student Data Disk

AppleWorks Word Processing is keyed to files on a disk furnished with the Teacher's Guide. Each student needs a copy of this disk while carrying out the hands-on activities at the computer.

Copiable disk A master copy of the Computer Applications Data disk is supplied with classroom sets of the workbook. Appendix B of the Teacher's Guide contains detailed instructions for making copies of the disk.

Purpose The Data disk solves a serious problem inherent in teaching word processing. Many word-processing techniques are best learned while interacting with a large text file; but many students, probably the majority, have poor keyboard skills. It is unrealistic to expect students to enter large files like these at the keyboard. The solution is to provide a disk with many sample files, each chosen to bring out an important point, and to key the workbook to the use of these files.

Student files The Data disk also gives students a place to store the files they are asked to create or edit as they proceed through the workbook. The files supplied on the Data disk occupy only about a third of the space available. Plenty of room is left for student files.

Other uses The master copy of the Data disk contains files for use with the AppleWorks word processor, data base, and spreadsheet programs. Only the word processor files are used with the present workbook. The other workbooks in this series (*AppleWorks Data Bases*, *AppleWorks Spreadsheets*, and *Hands-On AppleWorks*) are keyed to the remaining files on the Data disk. Having a single disk avoids a management problem for teachers who use several different workbooks in the series.

The Teacher's Guide

An extensive Teacher's Guide is provided at no cost with classroom sets of *AppleWorks Word Processing.* Features of the Teacher's Guide are described in the paragraphs below.

Key to computer literacy textbooks Some teachers may use this book in conjunction with a computer literacy textbook. Because most of these texts are weak with respect to specific hands-on activities for word processing, the contents of *AppleWorks Word Processing* have been keyed to popular computer texts now in use.

Hints for getting started The first-time teacher of a class that has a computer lab component faces serious management problems. The Teacher's Guide contains a full discussion of these problems and presents many hints designed to assure smooth operation throughout the class.

AppleWorks resources The Teacher's Guide contains a list of supplemental material of interest to AppleWorks users and teachers. This list includes periodicals, manuals, and information about user groups.

Discussion of each lab The largest part of the Teacher's Guide is devoted to a "play-by-play" discussion of each lab. This discussion includes a list of learning objectives, a description of what students will do in the lab, hints for avoiding problems in the labs, and suggestions for classroom follow-up.

Instructions for preparing disks Each student will need a copy of the Computer Applications Data disk, and there must also be a set of AppleWorks disks for each computer. Appendixes A and B of the Teacher's Guide contain detailed instructions for preparing these disks.

Answer sheets Answer space is provided after each question in the workbook. The most convenient way to use the workbook is to have students jot down answers in the workbook as they carry out their hands-on activities. For teachers who prefer to have the answers appear on separate sheets of paper, Appendix C of the Teacher's Guide contains answer sheet masters for the questions in each lab.

Transparency masters To aid the teacher in discussing hands-on lab activities, Appendix D of the Teacher's Guide contains a set of transparency masters that represent the important AppleWorks screens and other relevant information. These masters can be removed and reproduced as overhead transparencies.

The Luehrmann & Peckham Approach

Arthur Luehrmann and Herbert Peckham, the authors of this AppleWorks series, are well known to computer educators around the world. They are frequent speakers at computer education conferences and they have written two dozen textbooks on computing, many of which have been translated into French, Italian, Spanish, German, Portuguese, and Japanese.

Luehrmann & Peckham textbooks are in use at all levels from grade six to adult education. Their highly acclaimed junior high school text, *Computer Literacy—A Hands-On Approach,* has been used by over a million students since its publication in 1983. Several hundred thousand high school and college students have taken their first steps in Pascal via *Apple Pascal—A Hands-On Approach.* Peckham's *Hands-On BASIC* series is also widely used in schools and colleges. Apple Computer and IBM have packaged Luehrmann & Peckham tutorial manuals with their hardware and software.

Field-tested method The distinctive feature of all these works is the meticulous care with which the authors lead beginners through a sequence of concrete, hands-on experiences at the keyboard of a computer. This hands-on method, the result of decades of teaching experience, was finely honed during a national field test of the authors' material by a team from the School of Education at Stanford University. Over 600 students at 16 sites around the country were involved in the test, which took place in 1982.

In the new AppleWorks series of books, Luehrmann and Peckham apply their successful hands-on approach to teaching word processor, data base, and spreadsheet use to beginners. The authors believe that integration of the computer into the traditional curriculum will not occur until all students have practical computer skills. As always, therefore, their emphasis in the new series is on developing exciting skills in *using* the computer, not just reading dry facts.

Arthur Luehrmann A physicist by training, Luehrmann received his PhD from the University of Chicago in 1966. He began teaching at Dartmouth College at a time when educational computing was just beginning to become a reality, and he became a convert to this cause. In 1972 Luehrmann coined the phrase "computer literacy" and wrote and spoke widely of the importance of this new subject in the school curriculum. Before devoting full time to writing and publishing textbooks, he was Associate Director of the Lawrence Hall of Science at the University of California, Berkeley.

Herbert Peckham Another former physics teacher, Peckham is a graduate of the United States Military Academy. He received his master's degree from the Naval Postgraduate School and did additional work in physics at the University of California, Berkeley. He has taught physics, computer science, and mathematics at Gavilan College.

AppleWorks Word Processing is a guide for all your work at the computer as you learn about word processing. It will show you how to start the computer, how to give commands, how to use your disks, and how to correct mistakes. The book is divided into three chapters. Each chapter is made up of separate sections called labs. It should take about 30–45 minutes to complete a lab. If you run out of time, just save your work on your disk and continue later.

As you flip through the book, you will discover that most pages have parts that look like this:

Follow the Steps

● **Type today's date and tap the (RETURN) key.**

  If you make a mistake, use the (DELETE) key to erase it.

● **See what happens when you use the four arrow keys.**

● **Use the arrow keys to try to move the cursor off the bottom of the screen.**

These are examples of the instructions that you will carry out when you are at the computer. It is very important that you read each instruction carefully before you carry it out. The comments that follow some instructions are especially helpful when unexpected things happen. Be sure to read a comment before going on.

From time to time you will see parts of the book that look like this:

Read This

◆ **The AppleWorks disks** No computer system works without a **program**— a set of instructions to tell the computer exactly what to do. The AppleWorks program is too big to fit on a single disk, so it is divided into two main pieces. The first piece is on the AppleWorks Startup disk, and the second piece is on the AppleWorks Program disk. Both pieces must be loaded into the computer before AppleWorks can be used.

When you come to a part like this, you should turn away from the computer for a few moments and read. You will find that these parts usually help explain things that you have just finished doing at the computer. Many of your questions will be answered by reading these parts carefully. They are very short so that you can get back to the computer quickly.

At the end of most main sections, you will see this feature:

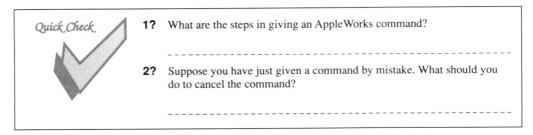

Quick Check

1? What are the steps in giving an AppleWorks command?

2? Suppose you have just given a command by mistake. What should you do to cancel the command?

These are examples of "quick-check" questions. Take a few moments to write short answers. If you have done all the steps at the computer, you will answer them easily.

Near the end of most labs you will discover a feature like this:

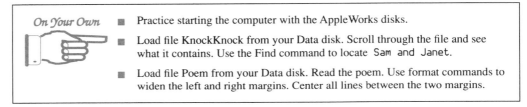

On Your Own

■ Practice starting the computer with the AppleWorks disks.

■ Load file KnockKnock from your Data disk. Scroll through the file and see what it contains. Use the Find command to locate Sam and Janet.

■ Load file Poem from your Data disk. Read the poem. Use format commands to widen the left and right margins. Center all lines between the two margins.

These are examples of On Your Own activities. They are things for you to do without being given any help. Doing these activities is the best test of whether you have actually learned the things covered in the lab.

At the very end of most labs you will find a list of review questions that cover all the things you did and read in the lab. You can write answers while in the lab or later. Review questions look like this:

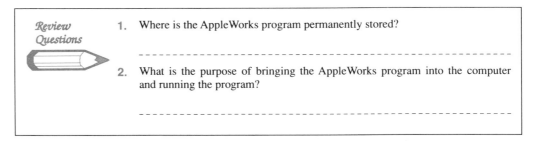

Review Questions

1. Where is the AppleWorks program permanently stored?

2. What is the purpose of bringing the AppleWorks program into the computer and running the program?

Finally, at the end of each chapter, the "Review and Glossary" gives definitions of all computer terms and commands introduced in the chapter.

Introduction to AppleWorks

Throughout this book you will be using the computer as a tool for writing. You will enter words at the keyboard, see them on the screen, make changes easily, and print the finished product on paper. The computer program that makes this possible is part of a package called AppleWorks.

◆ **What is AppleWorks?**   Three different application programs make up the complete AppleWorks package. The word processor program helps with the task of writing and is the program you will use in this book. AppleWorks also contains a data base program for working with large collections of information. Finally there is a spreadsheet program for doing calculations with tables of numbers.

◆ **Integrated package**   AppleWorks is an example of an integrated software package. This means that the three application programs that make up the package are designed to work together. Once you master the AppleWorks word processor program, you are well on your way to learning about the data base and spreadsheet programs that form the rest of the package.

◆ **General tools**   Because the package is integrated, many of the things you will learn in this book apply to all three parts of AppleWorks. Examples include starting the computer with the AppleWorks disks, giving commands, bringing information from a disk into the computer, making changes in the information, and saving your work on a disk. Chapter 1 introduces these basic tools. Chapters 2 and 3 deal with the special AppleWorks tools for working with words.

Goals
- ✔ Start the computer with the AppleWorks disks.
- ✔ Give commands contained on menus.
- ✔ End a session with AppleWorks.

The Apple II Computer System

◆
★

Throughout this book you will be using an Apple II computer system. If you have never used an Apple II, read the rest of this section. Otherwise skip ahead to the next page.

◆ **Main parts**   The Apple II computer system has four main parts: the **main unit** (a box containing electronic circuits), a typewriter **keyboard**, a television **monitor**, and at least one **disk drive**. There may also be a **printer**. On Apple IIe and IIc models, the keyboard is built into the front part of the main unit. On the Apple IIc, a disk drive is also built into the main unit; the disk drive door is on the right side.

◆ **Disks and drives**   You will be using several disks with your computer system. Be very careful when handling disks. Keep fingers, dust, and dirt away from the black plastic surface. Do not write on a disk or crease it. Do not put disks on top of the monitor or other electrical equipment. When placing a disk in a drive, open the drive door gently, slide the disk all the way in, and close the door all the way. (The drive door on the Apple IIc is opened by pressing in toward the main unit, not up.)

◆ **Power switches and lights**   Before you can use the computer system, the power to the main unit and the monitor must both be on. A light near the keyboard tells whether the main unit is on. Most monitors also have power-on lights. The main unit on-off switch is on the back; you can reach it with your left hand. The monitor on-off switch may be on the front, side, top, or back.

How to Start the Computer with AppleWorks

Before you can use any of the three application programs in AppleWorks, you must start the computer properly. You will need two disks for this computer lab: the AppleWorks Startup disk and the AppleWorks Program disk.

Starting AppleWorks   If you have separate instructions for starting your computer with AppleWorks, follow those instructions; if not, follow the instructions below.

Follow the Steps

● **1. Be sure the monitor is switched on and the (CAPS LOCK) key is in the UP position.**

The (CAPS LOCK) key is at the lower left corner of the keyboard.

● **2. Insert the disk labeled AppleWorks Startup into drive 1.**

On the Apple IIc, drive 1 is the built-in disk drive and drive 2, if present, is the external disk drive.

● **3. If the power to the main unit is off, just switch it on and skip the steps below. If the main unit power is already on, carry out the steps below:**

▲ **Hold down the (CONTROL) key (at the left edge of the keyboard).**

▲ **While the (CONTROL) key is down, hold down the open-apple key ⊙ (just left of the spacebar). Use your left hand to hold down both keys.**

▲ **While both keys are down, tap the (RESET) key. (On the Apple IIe, this key is at the upper right corner of the keyboard. On the Apple IIc, it is at the left above the keyboard. On the Apple IIGS, it is the large key above the regular keys.)**

▲ **Release all three keys.**

The disk drive's In Use light comes on as soon as you finish step 3. This tells you that the computer is reading the first part of the AppleWorks program from the disk.

When the light goes out, your screen should look like the figure below. (There may be small differences, depending on the version of AppleWorks you are using.)

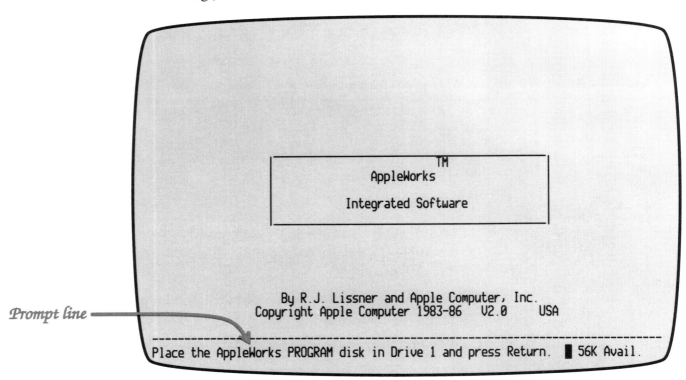

Prompt line

```
                                    TM
                              AppleWorks

                          Integrated Software




                By R.J. Lissner and Apple Computer, Inc.
                Copyright Apple Computer 1983-86   V2.0     USA
------------------------------------------------------------------------
Place the AppleWorks PROGRAM disk in Drive 1 and press Return.  █ 56K Avail.
```

The flashing cursor calls your attention to the instructions printed at the bottom of the screen. The AppleWorks program uses the bottom line of the screen to print **prompts**—messages that ask for information or tell you what to do next. This prompt leads to step 4.

● **4. Remove the Startup disk from drive 1 and set it aside. Locate the disk labeled AppleWorks Program. Insert this disk into drive 1. Then tap the (RETURN) key.**

Now the computer reads the final part of the AppleWorks program from the disk you just inserted.

When the disk drive light goes out, step 4 is complete. Your screen should look similar to this:

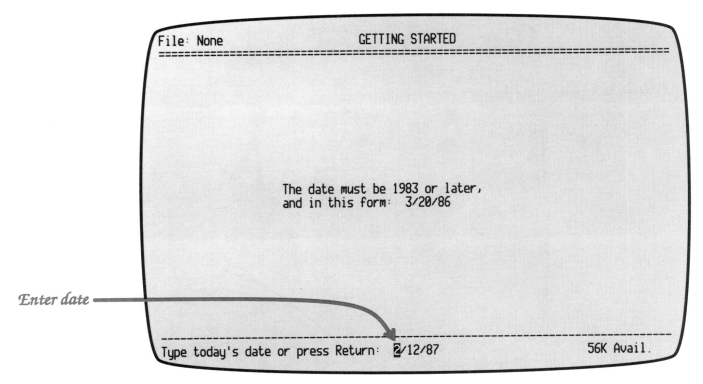

```
File: None                    GETTING STARTED
===============================================================================




                    The date must be 1983 or later,
                    and in this form:  3/20/86




Enter date ─────────────────────────────────────────────┐
                                                         │
  -------------------------------------------------------▼-----------------------
  Type today's date or press Return:  2/12/87                    56K Avail.
```

As before, the flashing cursor is at the bottom line, calling attention to the prompt there.

● **5. Type today's date in the form shown. Use the spacebar to remove any extra numbers.**

If you make a typing error, you can use the (DELETE) key to erase characters.

● **When the date is correct, tap (RETURN).**

The computer writes the new date on the Program disk. (The date helps identify whatever information you later save on a disk.)

As soon as you enter the date correctly, you should see an important screen with the title Main Menu.

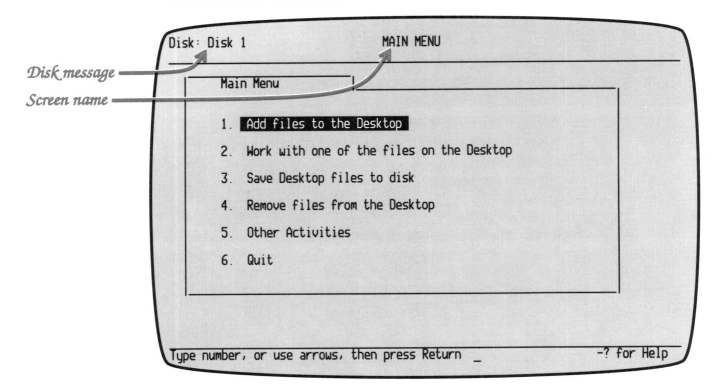

Disk message —
Screen name —

```
Disk: Disk 1                          MAIN MENU
────────────────────────────────────────────────────────────
    ┌─────Main Menu─────┐
    │                   │
    │
        1.  Add files to the Desktop

        2.  Work with one of the files on the Desktop

        3.  Save Desktop files to disk

        4.  Remove files from the Desktop

        5.  Other Activities

        6.  Quit



────────────────────────────────────────────────────────────
Type number, or use arrows, then press Return _      -? for Help
```

Most AppleWorks screens have names. This screen is called the Main Menu. (This screen may look slightly different on your computer.) When you see the Main Menu screen, you know you have started AppleWorks correctly.

● **6. Look at the upper left corner of the Main Menu screen. If your computer has only one disk drive, the phrase after** Disk: **should be either** Disk 1, Drive 1, Built-in disk, **or** Built-in drive. **If your computer has two drives, the phrase should be** Disk 2, Drive 2, Ext. disk, **or** Ext. drive.

Important!   If the phrase at the upper left corner of the Main Menu is wrong, your AppleWorks disks are set up for a different computer system. Ask for help in getting a proper set of disks.

After you have started the computer several times, the steps will become second nature. Now is a good time to review what you did.

◆ **The AppleWorks disks**   No computer works without a **program**—a set of instructions to tell the computer exactly what to do. The AppleWorks program is too big to fit on a single disk, so it is divided into two main pieces. The first piece is on the AppleWorks Startup disk, and the second piece is on the AppleWorks Program disk. Both pieces must be loaded into the computer before AppleWorks can be used.

◆ **Starting the computer**   These are the main steps you used to start the computer with AppleWorks:

1.   Switch the monitor on and make certain the (CAPS LOCK) key is up.

2.   Put the AppleWorks Startup disk in drive 1.

3.   Either switch the power on or, if it is already on, give the three-key command (CONTROL ⌂ RESET).

4.   Follow the instructions on the screen to insert the AppleWorks Program disk into drive 1. Then tap (RETURN).

5.   Follow the instructions on the screen to type today's date. Then tap (RETURN).

6.   Check the message at the upper left corner of the Main Menu. Make certain it is correct for the number of drives in your computer system.

These steps bring the AppleWorks program into the computer and start the program running. From then on, the AppleWorks program is in charge of your computer.

◆ **Screen prompts**   AppleWorks always prints a helpful prompt at the bottom of the screen. These prompts guide you safely through the steps needed to start the computer and carry out commands. There is no need to memorize all the steps. However, it *is* important to remember the first few steps of each task so that you will know how to begin.

Quick Check

1?   When you start AppleWorks, which disk should be in the drive first?

_____

2?   You know that you have started AppleWorks correctly when a certain screen appears. What is the name of that screen?

_____

Selecting Menu Commands

◆
★

If you have used a computer to write programs, you probably gave the computer commands by typing the name of the command on the keyboard and then tapping (RETURN). To use AppleWorks, you also need to give commands, but you do it differently.

The names of many AppleWorks commands are contained on lists called **menus**. The first step in giving a menu command is **selecting** its name. Whenever any menu item is selected, it is **highlighted**—the letters on the screen appear dark against a bright rectangle. At the present time, item 1 on the Main Menu is already selected.

● **Read the bottom line on the screen.**

● **Tap the ④ key.**

You have just selected menu item 4.

● **Tap the ⬇ key.**

Now menu item 5 is selected.

● **Tap the ⬆ key twice.**

Menu item 3 is selected.

● **Tap the ⬇ key until the last item on the menu is selected.**

● **Tap ⬇ once more.**

This "wraparound" effect is a quick way to get from the bottom of a menu to the top. Similarly, the ⬆ key takes you from the top menu item directly to the bottom one.

Quick Check

3?   How do you know which command in a menu is selected?

_____

4?   What are two ways to select a different menu command?

_____

Giving Menu Commands

So far you have seen how to *select* a command on a menu. To *give* a command, you first select it and then tap (RETURN).

● **Select the** Other Activities **command on the Main Menu.**

● **Tap** (RETURN).

That's all it takes to give any menu command. The Other Activities command tells the computer to display a list of seven new commands. The figure at the top of the facing page shows how your screen should look now.

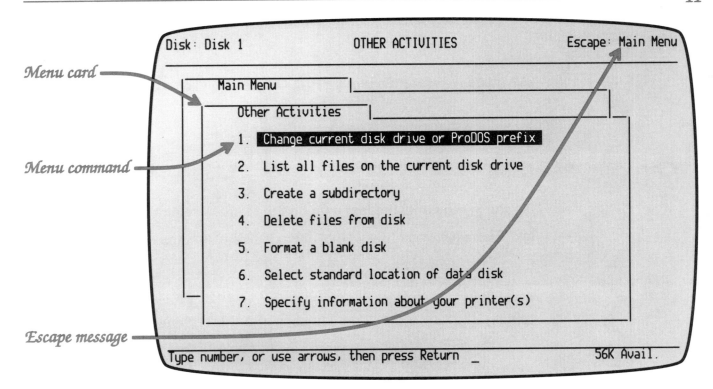

Menu card

Menu command

Escape message

```
Disk: Disk 1              OTHER ACTIVITIES          Escape: Main Menu

     Main Menu           |
        Other Activities    |
        1.  Change current disk drive or ProDOS prefix

        2.  List all files on the current disk drive

        3.  Create a subdirectory

        4.  Delete files from disk

        5.  Format a blank disk

        6.  Select standard location of data disk

        7.  Specify information about your printer(s)


Type number, or use arrows, then press Return _          56K Avail.
```

Each AppleWorks menu looks like an index card. The name of the menu is on the tab at the top, and the commands are listed on the face of the card. Some commands cause new menu cards to appear on top of cards already visible. Other commands remove menu cards from the stack.

The top item on the new menu is already selected. You can select other menu items on the new menu just as you did on the Main Menu. (This is true for all AppleWorks menus.)

● **Without tapping (RETURN), use the number keys to practice selecting menu commands.**

Notice that after you use a number key, you may not use another number key to make a different selection.

● **Practice using the arrow keys to highlight menu commands.**

Quick Check

5? How do you give a menu command?

_____

6? What does the `Other Activities` command on the Main Menu do?

_____

Changing Your Mind

◆
★

You are now looking at the seven possible commands on the Other Activities menu. Suppose that you don't want to give any of these commands. Instead you want to get back to the Main Menu and do something else.

Follow the Steps

● **Read the top line on the screen.**

The last part of the line says `Escape: Main Menu`.

● **Tap the** (ESC) **key at the upper left corner of the keyboard.**

The (ESC) key is the "escape" key. In AppleWorks you use this key to escape from where you are and go back to the previous menu. Notice that you are now back at the Main Menu.

● **Read the top line on the screen.**

Now there is no escape prompt at the end of the line.

● **Tap** (ESC).

The beep means that the key you tapped has no meaning here. In this case there is no previous menu. You can only go forward from the Main Menu.

● **Select menu item 1 and tap** (RETURN).

You have now given the `Add files...` command. This command causes a new menu to appear.

● **Tap** (ESC).

You have escaped from the Add Files menu and are now back at the Main Menu.

● **Give the** `Quit` **command and then use** (ESC) **to return to the Main Menu.**

Once again the (ESC) key cancels the command and returns to the previous screen. You should be back at the Main Menu now.

If you become confused about what to do when using AppleWorks, always look at the top and bottom lines of the screen before doing anything else. The top line always tells where you are in the AppleWorks program. (It may also tell you where you will go if you tap (ESC).) The bottom line contains the prompt message. On the Main Menu the prompt tells you how to enter a command.

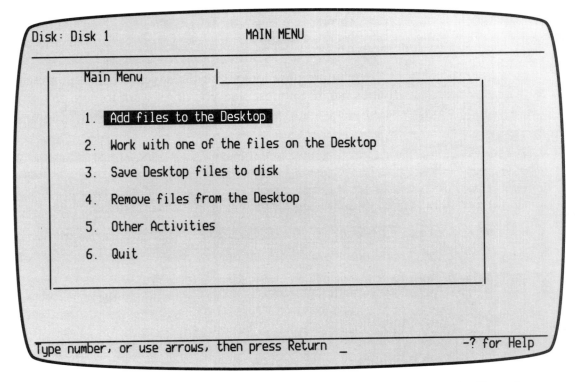

```
Disk: Disk 1                    MAIN MENU

    ┌─Main Menu──────────┐ ┌──────────────────────────┐
    │                    │ │
    │   1. █Add files to the Desktop█
    │
    │   2. Work with one of the files on the Desktop
    │
    │   3. Save Desktop files to disk
    │
    │   4. Remove files from the Desktop
    │
    │   5. Other Activities
    │
    │   6. Quit
    │

 Type number, or use arrows, then press Return _        -? for Help
```

◆ **Menu commands** The Main Menu is a list of six commands. You give a menu command by first selecting it from a menu and then tapping (RETURN). You select a command either by typing its number or by using the arrow keys to move down or up the menu. Commands that are selected always appear highlighted—that is, in dark type on a bright background.

◆ **The escape key** You can change your mind about most menu commands, even after tapping (RETURN), by tapping (ESC). This key allows you to escape from the command and go back to the menu that contains the command name. The (ESC) key also acts as the "Oops!" key: If you give a command by mistake, you can usually cancel the command by tapping (ESC).

◆ **Menus and trees** You can think of the AppleWorks menus as a tree structure. The Main Menu is the trunk. Other menus are branches. To reach a branch menu, you must always begin at the trunk and give the proper command to reach that branch. To get from one branch to another, you must first go back to the trunk by tapping (ESC).

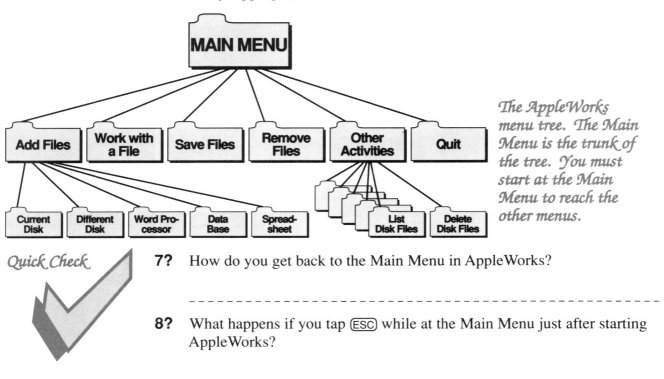

The AppleWorks menu tree. The Main Menu is the trunk of the tree. You must start at the Main Menu to reach the other menus.

Quick Check

7? How do you get back to the Main Menu in AppleWorks?

- -

8? What happens if you tap (ESC) while at the Main Menu just after starting AppleWorks?

- -

Quitting AppleWorks
◆
★

In this lab you have done things you will be doing again and again when using AppleWorks. Now it is time to leave AppleWorks in an orderly way.

● **If necessary return to the Main Menu.**

● **Give the** `Quit` **command.**

The prompt at the bottom of the screen asks if you really want to quit the program. If you selected `Quit` by accident, you could change your mind now.

● **Tap the** (Y) **key to confirm that you do want to quit.**

The `ENTER PREFIX` message at the top of the screen means that the AppleWorks program is no longer running in the computer.

● **Remove the AppleWorks Program disk from the drive. Return it and the AppleWorks Startup disk to their proper location.**

When you leave the computer, it is a good idea to leave the computer switched on if someone else will be using it within an hour or so. You should, however, switch the monitor off. This extends the life of the display screen.

Quick Check

9? What steps should you follow when quitting AppleWorks?

- -

10? Why does the computer ask you if you really want to quit?

- -

That completes your regular work in this lab. If you have time, carry out the On Your Own activities below. Be sure to quit AppleWorks properly.

On Your Own

■ Practice starting the computer with AppleWorks.

■ Go to the Other Activities menu. Give each of the seven commands there. Look at the new menu in each case. Then tap (ESC) to get back to the Other Activities menu. (WARNING: When you see each new menu, be sure to tap only the (ESC) key. Otherwise you may change or lose information on your disk.)

■ Practice quitting AppleWorks.

Review Questions

1. Where is the AppleWorks program permanently stored?

- -

2. What is the purpose of bringing the AppleWorks program into the computer and running the program?

- -

3. When you start the computer, you are asked to enter the date. How does AppleWorks make use of the date?

- -

4. Which key is always used to give a menu command?

- -

5. Which key usually cancels the previous menu command you gave?

- -

6. What does the top line on an AppleWorks screen tell you?

- -

7. What is a prompt, and where does it normally appear on the AppleWorks screen?

- -

★

Goals

✔ See the directory of files on a disk.

✔ Move an AppleWorks file from a disk into memory.

✔ Erase an AppleWorks file from memory.

Starting AppleWorks

◆
★

In this lab you will learn important commands for working with information stored on disks. Before doing that, however, you must start the computer with the two AppleWorks disks. You will also need your Computer Applications Data disk in this lab.

Follow the Steps

● **Carry out the steps below. (If you need more information, see pages 5–8 for details about each step.)**

▲ **1. If necessary switch the monitor on. Put the (CAPS LOCK) key in the UP position.**

▲ **2. Put the AppleWorks Startup disk in drive 1.**

▲ **3. Either switch the power on or give the three-key command (CONTROL|⌘|RESET).**

▲ **4. When prompted remove the AppleWorks Startup disk from the drive. Then insert the AppleWorks Program disk and tap (RETURN).**

▲ **5. When prompted type today's date and tap (RETURN).**

▲ **6. Check the message at the upper left corner of the Main Menu. Make certain it is correct for the number of drives in your computer system. If not ask for help.**

If all went well you should see the Main Menu on the screen. If not switch off the computer and start over. Recall that you can erase typing errors by using the (DELETE) key.

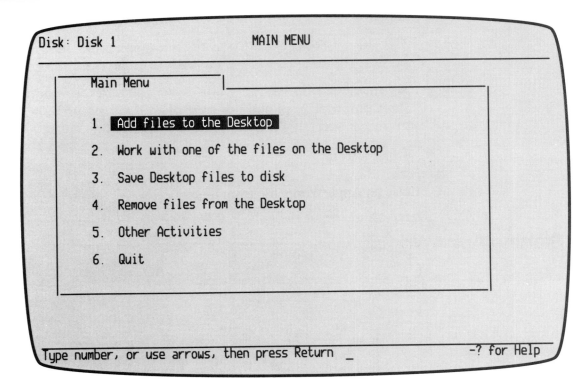

```
Disk: Disk 1                    MAIN MENU

   ┌─Main Menu──────────┬──────────────────────────┐
   │                    │                          │
   │  1. ▇Add files to the Desktop▇                │
   │                                               │
   │  2. Work with one of the files on the Desktop │
   │                                               │
   │  3. Save Desktop files to disk                │
   │                                               │
   │  4. Remove files from the Desktop             │
   │                                               │
   │  5. Other Activities                          │
   │                                               │
   │  6. Quit                                      │
   │                                               │
   └───────────────────────────────────────────────┘

  Type number, or use arrows, then press Return _        -? for Help
```

Looking at a Disk Directory

Your Computer Applications Data disk contains information grouped into separate collections called **files**. The first file command you will explore is the one for finding the names of all the files on a disk. Such a list of file names is called a **disk directory**.

Follow the Steps

● **Read the top line of the screen.**

The words at the upper left corner tell where AppleWorks expects you to put the disk you want to work with. Before long you will be putting your Data disk in this drive.

● **Use the arrow keys to highlight** Other Activities. **Then tap** (RETURN).

Recall that this is how you give a menu command. The Other Activities command tells the computer to display a new menu. Now there are two menu cards visible on the screen. Among the commands on the new menu is one that tells the computer to display a disk directory.

●   **Select the** List all files... **command. Tap** (RETURN).

Oops! Your Data disk is not yet inserted, so the directory cannot be displayed. The computer is waiting for you to put the disk into the proper drive.

●   **If your computer has only one drive, remove the Program disk and insert the Computer Applications Data disk. If your computer has two disk drives, insert the Data disk into drive 2.**

●   **Tap** (RETURN).

The List All Files menu card should now appear on top of the other two. It contains the directory for your Data disk. The directory shows the name, type, and size of each file, and the date and time the file was last changed.

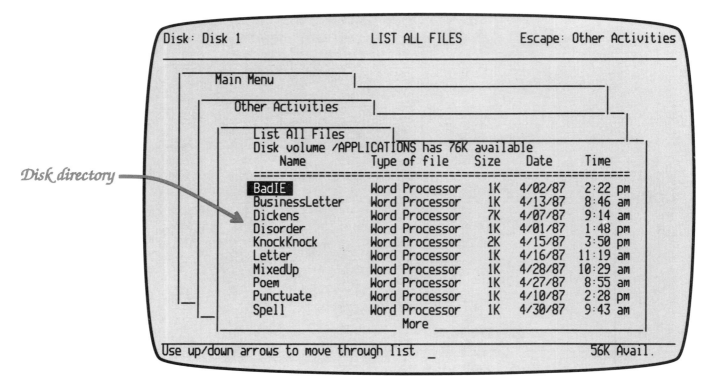

Disk directory

```
Disk: Disk 1                    LIST ALL FILES        Escape: Other Activities

    Main Menu
      Other Activities
        List All Files
        Disk volume /APPLICATIONS has 76K available
         Name            Type of file   Size    Date      Time
        =================================================================
        BadIE           Word Processor   1K    4/02/87    2:22 pm
        BusinessLetter  Word Processor   1K    4/13/87    8:46 am
        Dickens         Word Processor   7K    4/07/87    9:14 am
        Disorder        Word Processor   1K    4/01/87    1:48 pm
        KnockKnock      Word Processor   2K    4/15/87    3:50 pm
        Letter          Word Processor   1K    4/16/87   11:19 am
        MixedUp         Word Processor   1K    4/28/87   10:29 am
        Poem            Word Processor   1K    4/27/87    8:55 am
        Punctuate       Word Processor   1K    4/10/87    2:28 pm
        Spell           Word Processor   1K    4/30/87    9:43 am
                                More
Use up/down arrows to move through list  _              56K Avail.
```

●   **Find the word** More **at the bottom of the new menu card.**

You are looking at only part of the directory. The complete directory is too big to fit on the screen.

●   **Hold the** (↓) **key down until you hear a beep.**

By using the (↓) key, you can cause new file names to come into view as other names disappear. This is called **scrolling** through the directory.

●   **Hold the** (↑) **key down until you hear another beep.**

Now the file names at the beginning of the directory scroll into view. The (↓) key means "go toward the end" of the directory. The (↑) key means "go toward the beginning."

Chapter 1 introduces the six basic commands for working with Apple-Works files. You have now learned the first of these, the List all files... command.

◆ **The disk directory**   The file command you have been exploring is the one for listing the directory of a disk. These are the steps you used for seeing the directory of your Data disk:

1.   At the Main Menu, give the Other Activities command.

2.   At the Other Activities menu, and with the Data disk in the drive (drive 2 if you are using a two-drive system), give the List all files... command.

3.   If necessary, use the arrow keys to scroll through the directory.

The directory display shows the name, type, size, and date of last change for each file on your disk. When you started the computer with AppleWorks, you typed today's date. Whenever you make changes in a file and save it, the computer uses the date you typed as the date for that file. (If your computer has a clock installed, the time the file was saved will also be stored in the directory.)

◆ **Types of files**   You probably noticed that your Data disk contains three types of files. AppleWorks places all word processor files at the beginning of the directory, data base files in the middle, and spreadsheet files at the end. Files are alphabetized by name within each type. You will be using the word processor files for your work with this book.

1?   Which menu contains the command for showing the directory of a disk?

_____

2?   What information about a file does a disk directory contain?

_____

Bringing a File into Memory

The disk directory tells you the names of files on a disk. To see the file itself, you must first bring it into the computer's **memory unit**. The memory unit is where information is stored temporarily in the computer while you work on it. If you switch the power off, information in memory is lost.

Bringing a file into memory is called **loading** the file. Here is how to load an AppleWorks disk file into memory.

Follow the Steps

- ● **Use** ⒺⓈⒸ **to return to the Main Menu.**

- ● **Give the** Add files to the Desktop **command.**

    AppleWorks uses the word *Desktop* to stand for the computer's memory unit. A file in memory is said to be "on the Desktop." When you want to add files to the Desktop, AppleWorks gives you several options.

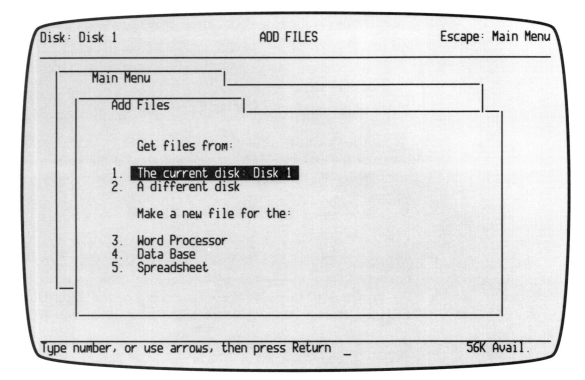

    The first two options are for loading a file from a disk. The last three are for creating a new file. Your goal now is to load a file from your Data disk. Command 1 is the proper option. The phrase at the end of the command tells where AppleWorks expects to find your Data disk. (The phrase you see on your screen may be different from the one shown in the figure.)

- ● **Give command 1 on the Add Files menu. If you are using a single-drive system, swap disks as prompted at the bottom of the screen.**

    The AppleWorks files menu shows you the directory of all files on your Data disk. (This is another way to see the directory.) For now ignore the prompt at the bottom of the screen. To load a file into memory you must first select the file name and then tap ⓇⒺⓉⓊⓇⓃ.

- ● **Use the** ⬇ **key to select file** Dickens. **Then tap** ⓇⒺⓉⓊⓇⓃ.

    The red disk drive light comes on, telling you that the computer is moving a copy of file Dickens into memory.

● **If prompted, insert the Program disk into the drive and tap (RETURN).**

When the move is complete, you see a new screen with the title Review/Add/Change. Part of the contents of the file Dickens appears on this screen.

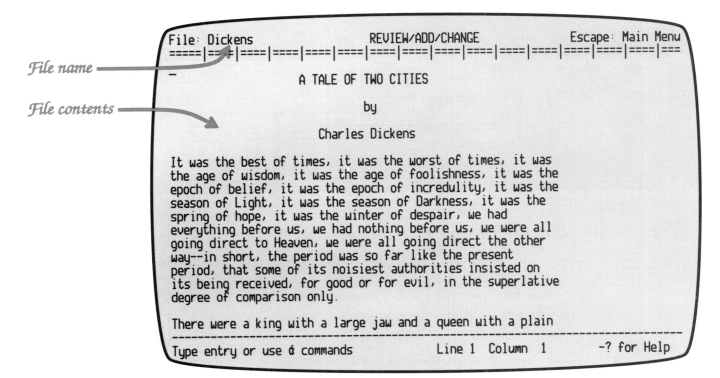

File name ——

File contents ——

```
File: Dickens                REVIEW/ADD/CHANGE           Escape: Main Menu
=====|====|====|====|====|====|====|====|====|====|====|====|====|====|===
-
                          A TALE OF TWO CITIES

                                  by

                            Charles Dickens

   It was the best of times, it was the worst of times, it was
   the age of wisdom, it was the age of foolishness, it was the
   epoch of belief, it was the epoch of incredulity, it was the
   season of Light, it was the season of Darkness, it was the
   spring of hope, it was the winter of despair, we had
   everything before us, we had nothing before us, we were all
   going direct to Heaven, we were all going direct the other
   way--in short, the period was so far like the present
   period, that some of its noisiest authorities insisted on
   its being received, for good or for evil, in the superlative
   degree of comparison only.

   There were a king with a large jaw and a queen with a plain
--------------------------------------------------------------------------
Type entry or use ⌨ commands         Line 1  Column 1      -? for Help
```

If you wished, you could now add, change, or delete information from this file and then save the new version on the disk. You'll learn more about these things in your next computer lab.

● **See what happens when you hold down each of the four arrow keys for a few seconds.**

The arrow keys move the cursor. Previously you used the (↑) and (↓) keys to scroll through a disk directory. You can also use these keys to scroll forward or backward through a file.

Now you have learned another file command. The new command tells the computer to load a file into memory. Here are the steps you used:

1. At the Main Menu, give the `Add files...` command.

2. At the Add Files menu, give the `From the current disk` command.

3. From the directory that appears, select the name of the file you want loaded. Then tap (RETURN).

If you are using a single-drive system, the computer will prompt you to swap disks when necessary.

◆ **The Review/Add/Change screen**   As soon as you load a file into memory, a copy of the file appears on the Review/Add/Change screen. (The original file remains on the disk.) This is a very important screen. Whenever you are entering or working with information in AppleWorks, you will be at a Review/Add/Change screen. Most of your time with AppleWorks will be spent at this screen.

Quick Check

3?   What steps are necessary to move a copy of a file from your disk into the computer's memory?

- -

4?   If you are told to swap disks, where do the instructions appear on the screen?

- -

Erasing a File from Memory

Now for a new file command. At the present time file Dickens is in memory. You can see a portion of it on the Review/Add/Change screen. Sooner or later you will want to remove the file from memory. The command for doing this is back on the Main Menu. The message at the upper right corner of the screen tells you what to do.

Follow the Steps

● **Tap (ESC) to go back to the Main Menu.**

This takes you back to the Main Menu as you wished. But suppose you had hit the (ESC) key by mistake while at the Review/Add/Change screen. There is an easy way to undo the mistake.

● **Tap (ESC) again.**

That takes you back to the Review/Add/Change screen and file Dickens is once more visible. Just leaving the Review/Add/Change screen does not remove a file from memory. You must give a specific command to do that.

● **Tap (ESC) once more.**

● **Read command 4.**

As already pointed out, the term *Desktop* stands for the computer's memory unit. Command 4 tells the computer to erase a file from its memory.

● **Give the** Remove files... **command.**

The Remove Files menu shows that Dickens is the only file now in memory. It is already selected. To delete it you need only tap (RETURN).

● **Tap** (RETURN).

The computer quickly erases the file from memory and returns to the Main Menu.

● **Try tapping** (ESC) **to return to the Review/Add/Change screen.**

It doesn't work since there is no file in memory now.

The third and last file command you have explored in this lab is the one for erasing a file from the computer's memory unit. You used these steps:

1. At the Main Menu, give the Remove files... command.

2. At the Remove Files menu, select the name of the file to be removed; then tap (RETURN).

These steps tell the computer to erase only the version of a file that is in the memory unit. The Remove files... command has no effect on disk files.

◆ **Other file commands**   So far you have learned three of the main Apple-Works commands for work with files. These are the commands for seeing a disk directory, loading a file into memory, and erasing a file from memory. Before you can use AppleWorks, however, you must learn three more file commands. In the next computer lab, you will learn to create a new file, save a file on a disk, and delete a file from a disk.

Quick Check

5?   What steps are necessary to erase an AppleWorks file from the computer's memory?

6?   What term is used in AppleWorks to refer to the computer's memory unit?

7?   Suppose you tap (ESC) by accident while working on a file at the Review/Add/Change screen. What will happen? What should you do to correct your mistake?

That completes your regular work in this lab. If you have time, do the On Your Own activities below. Then quit AppleWorks as shown on page 14.

On Your Own

■   Use the Add files... command on the Main Menu to load the data base file named Planets into the computer's memory. After you have looked at the file, remove it from memory.

■   See whether you can load two different files into memory at the same time. Explore command 2 on the Main Menu. Remove all files from memory.

Review Questions

1. What is a disk directory?

   ----

2. What AppleWorks command displays the disk directory? What menu has this command?

   ----

3. If you are at the Main Menu and want to load a disk file into memory, what command must you give?

   ----

4. On which screen can you see information stored in a file?

   ----

5. Suppose you have just finished loading a file into memory? Where else is the file?

   ----

6. Suppose you are looking at a file on the Review/Add/Change screen. You decide to erase the file from memory. What is the first key you should tap?

   ----

7. What does it mean to say that a file is "on the Desktop" in AppleWorks?

   ----

8. Suppose you have just loaded a file into memory from a disk. Then by accident you switch the power off. Does the file still exist anywhere? If so, where?

Goals

✔ Create a new AppleWorks file and enter information into it.
✔ Save a file on a disk and load it back into memory.
✔ Delete a file from a disk.

Creating an Empty File in Memory

In this lab you will create a new file in memory and enter information into it. Then you will save the file on your Data disk. Finally you will delete the file from your disk. These activities will introduce three new file commands. The first step is to start the computer with the two AppleWorks disks.

Follow the Steps

● **Start the computer with your AppleWorks disks. If you've forgotten the steps, see page 16.**

Your first task will be to create a new file to hold the information you will soon enter from the keyboard. You have already used the Add files... command to load a file into memory from a disk. The same command also allows you to create a new file. This command should now be highlighted on the Main Menu.

● **Tap (RETURN) to give the** Add files... **command.**

You have seen the Add Files menu before. The first two commands tell the computer to get files that are stored on a disk. The last three commands tell the computer to create a new file. The new file can be either a word processor file, a data base file, or a spreadsheet file. Here is how to create a new word processor file.

● **On the Add Files menu give command 3 to tell the computer to create a new word processor file.**

A third menu card appears on the screen. The new menu asks whether you want to make the new file from scratch or from an existing text file. *From scratch* means that you want a new file with nothing in it.

● **On the Word Processor menu give command 1 to create a new file from scratch.**

At this point your screen should look like the figure below. (The message at the upper left will vary, depending on how many drives you have and which version of AppleWorks you are using.)

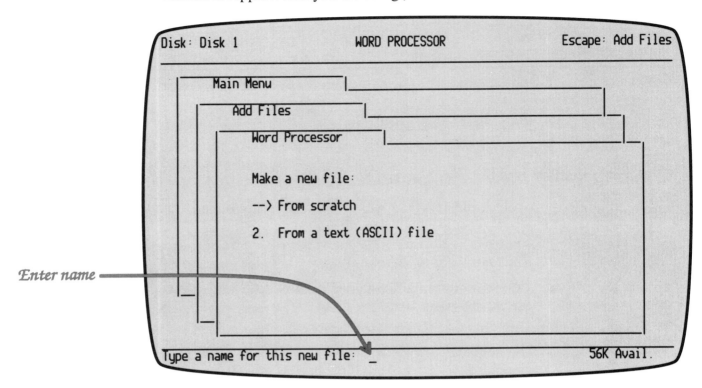

The prompt at the bottom of the screen tells you that the computer is waiting for you to give a name to the new file. AppleWorks requires all files to have names, even new files with nothing in them.

● **Type the name** MyText. **Use the** (DELETE) **key to erase any typing errors.**

● **When the name is correct, tap** (RETURN).

When you finish, the screen should look like the figure on the facing page. Your new file, named MyText, is now on the Desktop. You are at the Review/Add/Change screen. As you see, the file is empty.

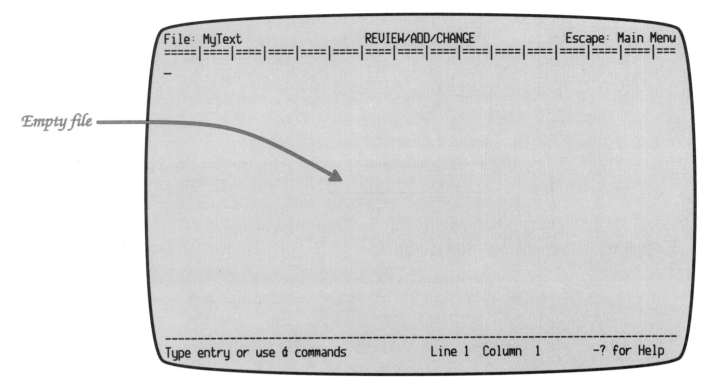

Empty file —————

```
File: MyText                    REVIEW/ADD/CHANGE              Escape: Main Menu
=====|====|====|====|====|====|====|====|====|====|====|====|====|====|====|===
_



















--------------------------------------------------------------------------
Type entry or use ⌐ commands              Line 1  Column  1          -? for Help
```

In the previous AppleWorks lab you learned three commands for working with files. They told the computer to display a disk directory, to load a file into memory, and to erase a file from memory. Now you have just learned how to make a new file from scratch. Here are the steps you used:

1. On the Main Menu, give the `Add files...` command.

2. On the Add Files menu, give the `Word Processor` command.

3. On the Word Processor menu, give the `From scratch` command.

4. Type a name for the file and tap (RETURN).

Creating a new data base file or a new spreadsheet file works almost the same way. The only difference is that in step 2 you would give the `Data Base` or `Spreadsheet` command instead of the `Word Processor` command.

◆   **Entering information**   As soon as the new file is created, AppleWorks displays the empty file on the Review/Add/Change screen. The cursor flashes at the top left corner of the blank part of the screen, waiting for you to enter information.

Quick Check

1?   Suppose you have just started AppleWorks. You want to enter information into a new file. What command on the Main Menu should you give?

_ _

2?   When creating a file, what does the term *from scratch* mean?

_ _

3?   How do you know that you have succeeded in creating a new file?

_ _

Entering Information into a File

◆
★

The Review/Add/Change screen is not a command menu; it is like a blank sheet of paper. The flashing cursor means that the computer is waiting for you to enter information.

Follow the Steps

● **Read the prompt line at the bottom of the screen.**

The computer tells you either to type something or to use ⓓ ("open-apple") commands. (Your prompt line will show either an open-apple symbol or a highlighted *A*. You'll learn about open-apple commands later.) For now your task is to enter information. Whatever you type will be stored in memory in the file named MyText.

● **Type the sentence below. Use** (DELETE) **to erase any mistakes.**

I am using a computer to type this sentence.

As you type each letter, the cursor moves to the right and the column number shown at the bottom of the screen changes.

● **Tap** (RETURN) **a few times.**

The new cursor position is shown at the bottom of the screen.

● **Type your name.**

You could go on adding hundreds or thousands of words to this file, but this small file is enough for you to learn how to save the information on your disk and later get it back into memory.

Quick Check

4? What AppleWorks screen allows you to enter information into a file?

- -

5? How can you tell where the cursor is located in a word processor file?

- -

Saving a File on a Disk

◆
★

The file you have created is on the Desktop (in the computer's memory). If you switched off the power to the computer, the information would be lost. To avoid this you need to **save** the file, that is, to move a copy of the file from the memory unit to a disk. You will be saving file MyText on your Computer Applications Data disk.

Follow the Steps

● **If you have a two-drive system, this is a good time to insert your Data disk into drive 2.**

If you have a one-drive system, the computer will prompt you when to swap disks.

To save file MyText on your Data disk, you need to use a command on the Main Menu.

● **Read the message at the upper right corner of the screen. Then tap (ESC).**

You are now back at the Main Menu. You may be wondering whether you have lost the information you just entered.

● **Again read the message at the upper right corner of the screen. Then tap (ESC).**

Nothing is lost. Remember that you can use (ESC) to go back and forth between the Review/Add/Change screen and the Main Menu.

● **Go back to the Main Menu and read command 3.**

Command 3 tells the computer to move a copy of your file to your disk.

● **Give the** Save Desktop... **command.**

The result is the Save Files menu, which looks similar to the figure below.

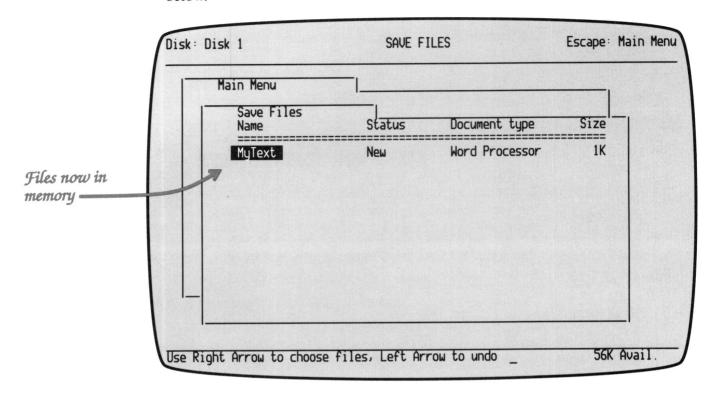

Files now in memory

This menu shows all files now on the Desktop. The new file MyText is the only one in memory now, so it is the only name that appears on the Save Files menu. The file name is already highlighted, so you need only tap (RETURN) to tell the computer you want the file saved.

● **Tap (RETURN).**

Now there is a third menu card on your screen, which should look like the figure on the facing page. The new menu confirms that you created file MyText and gives you two choices.

Command 1 is a little confusing. It would make more sense if it said "Save the file on the current *drive*." (The current drive is the one given in the message at the top of the screen.) Normally you want to save files on this drive, so command 1 is the right choice.

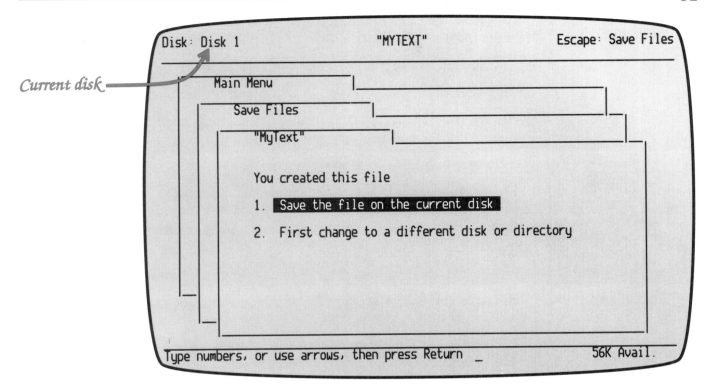

Current disk

Disk: Disk 1   "MYTEXT"   Escape: Save Files

Main Menu

Save Files

"MyText"

You created this file

1. Save the file on the current disk

2. First change to a different disk or directory

Type numbers, or use arrows, then press Return _   56K Avail.

- **Give command 1. If you are using a one-drive system, swap disks when prompted.**

  The red disk drive light comes on, showing that the computer is saving a copy of the file MyText on your Data disk. After the file is saved, the computer returns to the Main Menu. You can make certain that the file is saved by looking at the disk directory. You learned how to do this in your previous lab work.

- **Go to the Other Activities menu and give the** List all files... **command.**

  You should see the name MyText listed with the word processor files. This shows that the file was saved on your disk. Is the original version of file MyText still on the Desktop? Let's see.

- **Return to the Main Menu and give command 2.**

  The original version of the file is still in the computer's memory. Only a copy was moved to your Data disk. Since there is now a copy of file MyText on your disk, you can safely erase the original version from memory. You learned how to do this in your previous lab work.

- **Go back to the Main Menu and give the** Remove files... **command.**

● **At the Remove Files menu, tap** (RETURN) **to tell the computer to remove file MyText from the Desktop.**

Now file MyText exists in only one place: your Data disk.

● **Give the** Work with...files... **command on the Main Menu.**

The boxed message at the center of the screen confirms that the Desktop is cleared. No files are in memory now.

● **Read the prompt line and do what it says.**

You have now added a fifth command to your list of file commands. This new command tells the computer to save a file on a disk. Saving means making a copy of a file in memory and putting the copy on a disk. These are the steps you used:

1. At the Main Menu, give the Save Desktop... command.

2. At the Save Files menu, select the name of the file to be saved and tap (RETURN).

3. Give the command saying that you want the file to be saved on the "current disk" drive. Swap disks if prompted.

◆ **The current drive**   In AppleWorks, files are normally saved on the disk in the "current drive." On a one-drive system, the current drive is drive 1 (the built-in drive on an Apple IIc). On a two-drive system, the Program disk stays in drive 1, so drive 2 (the external drive on an Apple IIc) is used as the current drive. Thus with two disk drives, there is no need to swap disks.

◆ **Saving means copying**   You discovered that the Save Desktop... command moves only a copy of the file to the disk. It is worth repeating that the original version remains in memory in case you want to return to the Review/Add/Change screen and work on it some more.

6?   Which menu contains the Save Desktop... command?

_____

7?   What does *save a file* mean?

_____

8?   After you save a file, it is on your disk. Where else is it?

_____

Loading File MyText from the Disk

◆
★

The file MyText that you created is no longer on the Desktop, but a copy is still on your disk. Next let's bring a copy of the file back into memory. You learned how to do this in your previous work at the computer.

Follow the Steps

● **Give the** `Add files...` **command on the Main Menu.**

● **Give command 1 on the Add Files menu. If you are using a one-drive system, swap disks when prompted.**

● **Use** ⬇ **to select** `MyText`. **Then tap** `RETURN`.

There is a short wait while the computer moves a copy of file MyText from your disk into the computer's memory unit. The information you saved is again visible on the Review/Add/Change screen. Is it also still on the disk?

● **Go to the main menu and give the** `Other Activities` **command. Then give the** `List all files...` **command.**

As you can see, file MyText is still on your Data disk.

Quick Check

9? What does *load a file from a disk* mean?

10? Just after loading a file, in what two places does the file exist?

Removing a File from the Disk

◆
★

Once again identical copies of file MyText appear in two places: on the Desktop and on your disk. Next you'll see how to erase the copy on the disk.

Follow the Steps

● **Go back to the Other Activities menu.**

● **Give the** `Delete files...` **command.**

Once again you see the directory of your disk. The computer is waiting for you to select the file you wish to delete.

● **Select** `MyText` **and tap** `RETURN`.

At the bottom of the screen the computer asks whether you *really* want to do this, since the file will be erased permanently from the disk. Your screen should look like the figure on the next page.

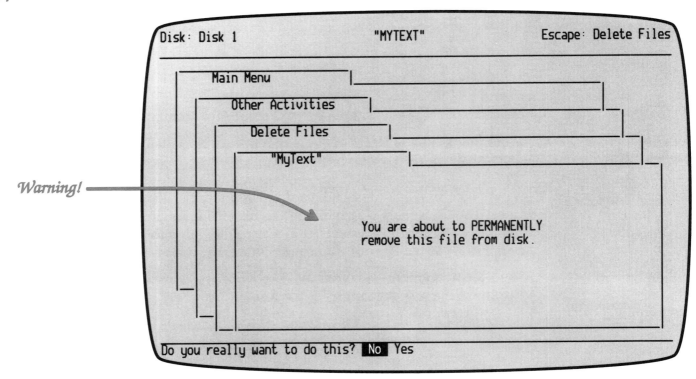

Warning!

● **Tap Ⓨ to confirm that you do want to delete the file.**

The red disk drive light comes on as the computer erases file MyText from the disk. After that, AppleWorks returns to the Other Activities menu.

● **Give the** `List all files...` **command on the Other Activities menu.**

The new directory shows that file MyText is no longer on the Data disk. Is it also gone from the memory unit?

● **Tap ⒺⓈⒸ twice to get back to the Main Menu.**

● **Give command 2 on the Main Menu.**

That returns you directly to the Review/Add/Change screen. Are you surprised to see the copy of file MyText still on the Desktop? The disk copy is gone, but the Desktop copy is still in the computer's memory. If necessary you could save a copy of MyText on the disk again.

The `Delete files...` command is the last of the six main commands needed for your work with AppleWorks files. This last command tells the computer to remove a file from a disk. Here are the steps you used to delete a saved file from the disk in the current drive:

1. At the Other Activities menu, give the `Delete files...` command.

2. Select the name of the file to be removed. Then tap ⓇⒺⓉⓊⓇⓃ.

3. Tap Ⓨ to confirm that you really do want the file to be removed.

You discovered in the lab that the Delete files... command has no effect on a file in the computer's memory unit. Only disk files can be erased by this command.

◆ **Help for the user**   The last step above is a nice example of **user friendliness**. The writer of this program knew that deleting a disk file is permanent. So the writer had the computer pause and ask you to make certain that the selected file should really disappear from the disk. This pause gives you a chance to change your mind before any damage is done.

◆ **A possible confusion**   Two AppleWorks commands, Delete files... and Remove files..., sound very much alike, but they do very different things. The first erases disk files and the second erases files in memory. *Since both commands erase information, it is important to make sure you are using the correct one.* The best way to avoid errors is to remember these commands by the menus they appear on: To erase a disk file, you must go to the Other Activities menu; to erase a file in memory, you need go only to the Main Menu.

Quick Check

11?   What does *delete a file from a disk* mean?

- -

12?   What menu contains the command for deleting a file from a disk?

- -

Quitting AppleWorks

◆
★

Now you have learned all the important commands for working with AppleWorks data files. If you have time, try some of the On Your Own activities on the next page. Then use these steps to leave AppleWorks:

● **Return to the Main Menu and give the** Quit **command. Tap ⓨ to confirm that you really want to quit.**

If you have changed a file since you last saved it, the computer will ask you what you want to do with the new version.

● **If prompted tell the computer to throw out any changes you do not want to keep. Tap ⓨ to confirm that you really want to throw out the changes.**

● **If prompted swap disks and tap** (RETURN).

The ENTER PREFIX message at the top of the screen means that the AppleWorks program is no longer running.

● **Remove the AppleWorks Program disk from its drive. Return it and the AppleWorks Startup disk to their proper location.**

● **Take your Computer Applications Data disk with you.**

On Your Own      ■ Practice quitting AppleWorks and restarting the computer with AppleWorks.

■ Restart AppleWorks. Use the Add files... command on the Main Menu to look at other files on your Computer Applications Data disk. When you are through looking at a file, remove it from the Desktop.

■ Create a new word processor file. Give it any name you choose. Enter any information you want into the file. Practice saving the file on your disk, looking at the disk directory, deleting the file from the disk, and removing the file from the Desktop.

Review Questions

1. What command allows you to create an empty file in the computer's memory?

   ----

2. What does the term *from scratch* mean?

   ----

3. What is the last step in creating a new, empty file in AppleWorks?

   ----

4. What AppleWorks command allows you to move a copy of a file from memory to a disk?

   ----

5. Which menu contains the AppleWorks command for erasing a file on a disk?

   ----

6. What two purposes does the Add files... command serve?

Main Menu Commands

Add files...	Move a copy of a file from a disk into the computer's memory or create a new file from scratch.
Other Activities	Choose a new menu containing additional AppleWorks commands.
Quit	End all AppleWorks activities.
Remove files...	Erase the copy of a file in the computer's memory. The disk copy, if any, is not affected.
Save Desktop...	Move a copy of a file from the computer's memory to a disk.
Work with...files...	Continue working with a file already in the computer's memory.

Other Activities Menu Commands

Delete files...	Erase a file permanently from a disk.
List all files...	Display a directory of files on a disk.

Keyboard Commands

DELETE	Erase the character just left of the cursor position.
ESC	In most cases, undo the effect of the previous command and return to the menu on which the command appeared.
RETURN	In most cases, issue a command or mark the end of an entry.
⌘	Not actually a command. This key is used with other keys to give special commands.
↑, ↓	Move the cursor up or down a line.
→, ←	Move the cursor right or left one character.

New Ideas

AppleWorks	An integrated software package consisting of a word processor program, a data base program, and a spreadsheet program.
data base	A collection of information organized to make it easy to search.

data base program	An application program that helps you organize and search through a collection of information.
Desktop	The name used by AppleWorks to refer to the computer's memory. A file loaded into memory is said to be "added to the Desktop."
disk directory	A list of information about the files stored on a disk.
file	A collection of information stored under a single name, either on a disk or in the computer's memory unit.
highlighted text	Text displayed on the screen as dark letters against a bright background.
integrated software package	A set of computer programs designed to be used together. AppleWorks is an integrated software package. In an integrated package, many of the same commands can be used with each program.
load a file	Move a copy of a file from a disk into the computer's memory unit.
memory unit	The part of a computer where information is stored temporarily while it is being processed. Information in memory is lost when power is switched off. AppleWorks refers to the memory unit as the "Desktop."
menu	A list of commands; a command is given by selecting it and tapping the (RETURN) key.
prompt	A message on the screen telling the user what can or should be done next.
Review/Add/Change screen	The screen on which text is entered into an AppleWorks file, deleted from the file, or changed.
save a file	Make a copy of a file in the computer's memory unit and write the copy on a disk.
scroll	Move information up or down on the screen in order to bring new lines into view.
select	Move the cursor to an AppleWorks command name. Selected commands are highlighted.
spreadsheet	A sheet of paper containing information arranged in rows and columns.
spreadsheet program	An application program that helps you do calculations on data stored in cells.
user-friendly software	Programs that give prompts, offer help to the user, and steer the user away from common mistakes.
word processing	Writing, editing, formatting, and printing text.
word processor program	An application program that helps you enter, edit, and print text.

Text Entry and Editing

Chapter 1 introduced you to the basic features of AppleWorks. You learned how to start the computer with AppleWorks, how to give commands, and how to enter information into the computer. You found that information is stored in files, and you explored all the basic commands for working with files.

◆ **The word processor program** Chapter 2 focuses on the word processor program in AppleWorks. This program turns your computer into a "smart typewriter." You enter words into a file just by typing them on the keyboard. After that, special word processor commands make it a simple task to scroll through your text, search for a word or phrase, and make changes in what you have written.

◆ **The writing task** For most people the hardest part of writing is making changes. Without a computer that means having to erase or scratch out words and then pencil in new words. After a few changes the paper looks messy. You may have to rewrite or retype the whole paper several times. It is easy to become discouraged and give up, even when you know that more changes are needed.

◆ **Word processor tools** With a word processor program, however, you can easily make any changes you want whenever you want. You simply use word processor commands to find the place that needs work. It takes only a few key strokes to delete phrases, sentences, or paragraphs. Then you enter the new material at the keyboard. When you are satisfied with the result, you can print a fresh copy of the new version. In the chapter ahead, you will learn the Apple-Works tools for doing all these things.

★

Goals

✔ Enter text into an empty word processor file.
✔ Insert and delete words in a word processor file.
✔ Use insert mode and exchange mode for entering text.

Creating an Empty Word Processor File

In this lab you will learn how to use the word processor program in AppleWorks to change, add, and delete information in a file. This process is called **editing**. To learn about editing, you will need a file to practice on. Begin by creating a new file named Speech and entering a few words into the file.

Follow the Steps

● **Start the computer with the AppleWorks disks.**

● **If you are using a two-drive system, now is a good time to insert your Data disk into drive 2.**

If all went well, you should see the Main Menu on the screen. The first command, Add files..., is already selected. There are no files in memory (on the Desktop) when you start AppleWorks, so your first task is to create file Speech. Here are the steps.

● **Tap** (RETURN) **to give the** Add files... **command.**

Remember that you can tap (ESC) if you give the wrong command. You want to create a new word processor file from scratch.

● **Give command 3 on the Add Files menu.**

This command tells the computer that you want to create a word processor file. (Commands 4 and 5 are the starting points for creating data base and spreadsheet files.)

● **Give command 1 on the Word Processor menu.**

As soon as you tap (RETURN), your screen should look like the figure on the facing page.

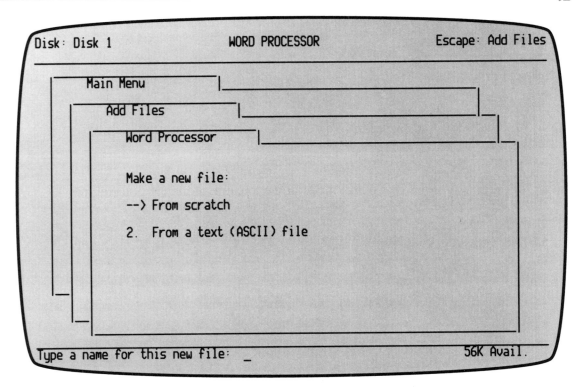

As usual the prompt at the bottom of the screen tells you what needs to be done next. To create a new file, you must give it a name.

● **Type the name** Speech. **If you make mistakes, use** (DELETE) **to erase them. When finished, tap** (RETURN).

Quick Check

1?   Which command on the Main Menu should you use to create a new file?

_____

2?   When you create a new file, on what screen does the empty file appear?

_____

Entering Text into the New File

◆
★

Your new file, named Speech, is now on the Desktop. You are at the Review/Add/Change screen. The flashing cursor at line 1, column 1, tells you that the computer is waiting for you to enter information into your empty file.

Follow the Steps

● **Type the following sentence. Be sure *not* to tap** (RETURN) **at the end of each line.**

A number of years ago, some folks started a
country that believed people were OK.

When you finish entering the sentence, the top part of your screen should look like the figure below. (If there are errors, use (DELETE) to erase them; then retype the rest.)

```
File: Speech              REVIEW/ADD/CHANGE           Escape: Main Menu
=====|====|====|====|====|====|====|====|====|====|====|====|====|====|===
A number of years ago, some folks started a country that
believed people were OK._
```

◆ **Wordwrap** If you were typing this sentence on a typewriter, you would have to watch each line and tap (RETURN) when the line got too long. With a word processor program, you don't have to do this. Computers often use a process called **wordwrap**. When a word is too long to fit on the current line, the computer moves the whole word to the beginning of the next line.

◆ **The RETURN key** There are only two times when you'll need to use (RETURN) while using a word processor program. When you reach the end of a paragraph, you should tap (RETURN), and when you want blank lines in your text, you enter them simply by tapping (RETURN) as many times as needed.

3? Why should you *not* use (RETURN) while typing a paragraph into a word processor file?

- -

4? When *should* you use (RETURN) while entering text into a word processor file?

- -

Inserting Words

After you've written something, you usually think of ways to improve it. Normally this means rewriting or retyping everything. With a word processor program, however, all you need to do is add new words or remove old words. No retyping is necessary. For example, here is how to add the word all before the word people in your sentence.

● **Tap ⊖ several times until the cursor is under the first letter of** people.

● **Type the word** all. **(Use (DELETE) to fix errors.) Then tap the spacebar to add a space.**

That's all there is to adding words. You **insert** new words by moving the cursor where you want the new words to start and then typing them.

Here is how the upper part of your Review/Add/Change screen should look now:

```
File: Speech                    REVIEW/ADD/CHANGE            Escape: Main Menu
=====|====|====|====|====|====|====|====|====|====|====|====|====|====|====|===
A number of years ago, some folks started a country that
believed all people were OK.
```

"all" inserted ———

You have now inserted the word `all` and a space into the sentence. Next insert a whole phrase.

- **Use the arrow keys to move the cursor under the the first letter in** `folks`. **Be sure not to use** (RETURN) **to move the cursor.**

- **Type the words** `pretty terrific` **and a space.**

You have changed `folks` to `pretty terrific folks`. As you see, inserting words or phrases gives you a simple tool for making changes in what you have written. You can also insert whole sentences or paragraphs in the same way: Just place the cursor where you want the new text to appear and enter the new material.

When editing a file you should save your work every few minutes. This protects against accidental losses. You learned one way to save a file on a disk in Chapter 1. Here is a shortcut:

- **Hold down the** (d) **key (just left of the spacebar) and tap** (S).

The Save command (d)(S) is an example of an open-apple command. (You will learn many more open-apple commands in this chapter.) The Save command tells the computer to make a copy of the file you are editing and put the copy on a disk.

- **If prompted follow directions for swapping disks.**

Be careful when using the (d)(S) shortcut for saving a file. This command is easier to use than the Main Menu `Save Desktop...` command. If a file with the same name as the one you are editing is already on the Data disk, however, the Main Menu command warns you and asks whether to go ahead. There is no warning with the (d)(S) command.

Quick Check

5? What keys move the cursor without affecting the words in the file?

- -

6? How would you insert the word *junk* just ahead of the word *food* in a word processor file?

- -

Deleting Words

You have seen how to insert new text. Next you will see how to get rid of unwanted text. This process is called **deletion**. Here's how to delete pretty from the sentence.

Follow the Steps

● **Move the cursor under the space after** pretty. **Use the** (DELETE) **key to erase** pretty **and the space before it.**

That's all there is to it. To delete text, place the cursor just after the text you want to delete. Then use (DELETE) to erase what you want. Here is what the top part of your screen should look like now:

```
File: Speech                   REVIEW/ADD/CHANGE              Escape: Main Menu
=====|====|====|====|====|====|====|====|====|====|====|====|====|===
A number of years ago, some terrific folks started a country
that believed all people were OK.
```

"pretty" deleted ————

Quick Check

7? Suppose the cursor is at the letter *r* in the word *years*. You tap (DELETE) once. What character is erased from your file?

_ _

8? Suppose you want to delete the word *cat* from your file. Where should the cursor be before you begin tapping (DELETE)?

_ _

Edit Modes

AppleWorks allows you to enter text from the keyboard in two different ways. These are called **edit modes**. You have been using the **insert mode** in your work so far. Now explore the other mode.

Follow the Steps

● **Put the cursor under the first letter of** started. **Notice the shape of the cursor.**

● **Hold down** (⌘) **and tap** (E). **Notice the new cursor shape.**

The Edit command (⌘E) is another example of an open-apple command. The Edit command switches from insert mode to a different mode called **exchange mode**. See how the new mode works.

● **Type the letters** crea **to exchange characters.**

In exchange mode each letter you type takes the place of a letter on the screen. The letters `crea` replaced `star`. You have changed the word `start-ed` into the word `created`.

● **Give the Edit command ⌧E again. Note the cursor shape.**

Now you are back in insert mode. This is a good time to save your work.

● **Give the Save commmand ⌧S.**

◆ **Edit modes**   As you have seen, AppleWorks gives you two different ways of entering text into the computer. In insert mode any letter you type is inserted at the cursor position. Characters beyond the cursor move to the right to make room. In exchange mode the letters you type replace letters already on the screen.

◆ **Cursor symbol**   How can you tell which mode AppleWorks is in? The answer is simple: Just look at the cursor. In insert mode the cursor is an underline symbol; in exchange mode the cursor is a solid rectangle.

◆ **Changing modes**   Switching between the two edit modes is easy. The Edit command ⌧E is the switch. If Appleworks is in insert mode, ⌧E switches to exchange mode. If it is in exchange mode, ⌧E switches to insert mode. You can give the Edit command whenever the cursor is visible.

◆ **Which mode is best?**   The exchange mode is useful for certain tasks, such as capitalizing a word that was written in lowercase, but accidents cause more damage in exchange mode than in insert mode. If you accidentally type a letter while in exchange mode, you *delete* the character at the cursor position and replace it with the new letter. In insert mode no characters are deleted. Instead the characters to the right move over and the accidental character is inserted. Tap ⌧DELETE and the error is fixed. To avoid accidents like this it is usually better to use insert mode.

9?   What command do you use to switch between insert mode and exchange mode?

- -

10?   How can you tell whether the computer is in insert mode or exchange mode?

- -

11?   What is the danger in using the exchange mode for editing text?

- -

Changing Words

◆
★

Follow the
Steps

You now know how to use the two main tools for editing text: You can *delete* words you don't want and *insert* new words. In this way you can make changes without retyping everything. You'll be using these editing tools again and again, so this is a good time to get some practice.

● **Use the steps below to change** people were OK **to** men are created equal

  ▲ **Place the cursor under the period after** OK

  ▲ **Delete** people were OK

  ▲ **Type** men are created equal

That's all there is to changing old words to new words. You simply delete the old words and type the new words.

● **Use the same method to change** some terrific folks **to** our fathers

● **Change** that believed **to the following phrase:**

  dedicated to the proposition that

After these changes, the top part of your screen should look like this:

```
File: Speech                    REVIEW/ADD/CHANGE            Escape: Main Menu
=====|====|====|====|====|====|====|====|====|====|====|====|====|====|====|===
A number of years ago, our fathers created a country
dedicated to the proposition that_all men are created equal.
```

● **In the top line change** created **to the phrase below. Remember, don't use** (RETURN).

  brought forth on this continent

● **Change** country **to the following phrase:**

  new nation, conceived in Liberty, and

● **Change** A number of **to this phrase:**

  Four score and seven

● **Use the arrow keys to move the cursor just after the period at the end of the sentence.**

● **Tap** (RETURN) **twice. Type** Abraham Lincoln

After all these changes you should see a familiar quotation on the top part of your screen.

```
File: Speech                    REVIEW/ADD/CHANGE              Escape: Main Menu
=====|====|====|====|====|====|====|====|====|====|====|====|====|====|====|===
Four score and seven years ago, our fathers brought forth on
this continent a new nation, conceived in Liberty, and
dedicated to the proposition that all men are created equal.

Abraham Lincoln_
```

● **If your screen looks different, use insertion and deletion to fix errors.**

● **If necessary move the cursor to the right of** Lincoln **Then tap** (RETURN) **three times. Type the following sentence:**

> I used a word processor program to write this.

● **Tap** (RETURN) **twice and type your name.**

This completes the editing job. You have entered text into the computer, inserted new material, and deleted unwanted material. Now it is time to save the final version of file Speech.

● **Give the Save command and swaps disks if prompted.**

Quick Check

12? When using a word processor program, what two things do you need to know how to do to change one word into another word?

_ _

13? What are the steps for changing one phrase into another phrase?

_ _

This completes the regular work in this lab. If you have time, do the On Your Own activities below. Then quit AppleWorks as usual.

On Your Own

■ Use the Remove files... command from the Main Menu to clear your Desktop. Then use the Add files... command to get file Spell from your Computer Applications Data disk. Find all the misspelled words you can and change each one to the correct spelling. Use the Name command (⌘N) to change the file name to SpellOK. Use the Save Desktop... command to save the improved version.

■ Clear your Desktop and load file Punctuate from your Computer Applications Data disk. The text you see has no punctuation or capital letters. Insert whatever punctuation is needed. Use exchange mode and capitalize any letters that need it. Use the Name command (⌘N) to change the file name to PunctuateOK. Save the corrected version.

■ Clear your Desktop. Create a new word processor file. Give the file the name MyThoughts. Write a few sentences that tell what you think about using a word processor program on a computer. Save the file.

1. Why is word processor editing preferable to pencil-and-paper methods?

    ----

2. When using a word processor program, what basic tools are needed to edit text?

    ----

3. At what AppleWorks screen must you be to insert or delete text in a word processor file?

    ----

4. In AppleWorks how do you delete a word from a file?

    ----

5. In AppleWorks how do you insert a word at a particular place in a file?

    ----

6. What does *wordwrap* mean?

    ----

7. What are two ways to save an AppleWorks file on a disk?

    ----

8. Suppose you try to save file MyText and your disk already contains a file with this name. What will happen if you use the Save command ⌘S?

    ----

9. What is the danger in using the exchange mode when editing a file?

★

Goals

✔ Send a copy of a word processor file to a printer.
✔ Scroll the text of a long file up and down the screen.
✔ Use keyboard commands to move the cursor quickly to any part of a file.

Printing a File

This lab has two parts. In the first part you will learn how to print a file. The second part shows how to work with a large file on the Review/Add/Change screen.

● **Start the computer with AppleWorks in the usual way.**

When you finish work on a word processor file, you usually want to make a **hard copy**—that is, to print the file on paper. If there is a printer attached to your computer, you can print any word processor file saved on your Data disk. (If not you will have to take your disk to another computer that has a printer attached.)

You will make a printed copy of file Speech, which you created and saved in the previous lab.

● **If you are using a two-drive system, insert your Data disk into drive 2 now.**

If you are using a single-drive system, the computer will soon prompt you to swap disks when your Data disk is needed.

The first step in printing an AppleWorks file is to load the file into the computer's memory.

● **Give the command** Add files... **on the Main Menu.**

● **Give the command** The current disk... **on the Add Files menu. If you are using a single-drive system, now is the time to swap disks and tap** (RETURN).

As usual when loading a file, the computer first displays the directory of your Data disk so that you can choose the file you want loaded.

Your screen should look like the figure below. The word processor files appear at the beginning of the directory and are listed in alphabetical order.

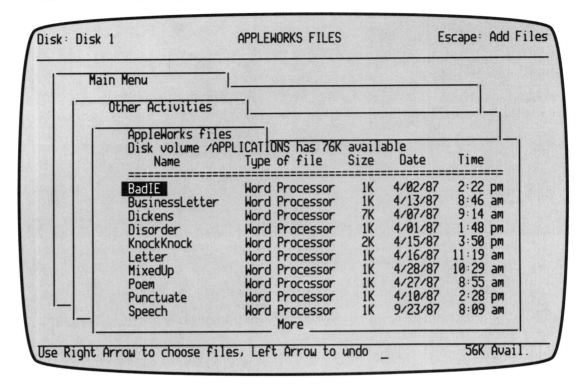

```
Disk: Disk 1              APPLEWORKS FILES              Escape: Add Files

     Main Menu          |
        Other Activities          |
          AppleWorks files          |
          Disk volume /APPLICATIONS has 76K available
             Name           Type of file   Size   Date     Time
          ========================================================
             BadIE          Word Processor   1K   4/02/87   2:22 pm
             BusinessLetter Word Processor   1K   4/13/87   8:46 am
             Dickens        Word Processor   7K   4/07/87   9:14 am
             Disorder       Word Processor   1K   4/01/87   1:48 pm
             KnockKnock     Word Processor   2K   4/15/87   3:50 pm
             Letter         Word Processor   1K   4/16/87  11:19 am
             MixedUp        Word Processor   1K   4/28/87  10:29 am
             Poem           Word Processor   1K   4/27/87   8:55 am
             Punctuate      Word Processor   1K   4/10/87   2:28 pm
             Speech         Word Processor   1K   9/23/87   8:09 am
                                   More
Use Right Arrow to choose files, Left Arrow to undo  _        56K Avail.
```

● **Locate file Speech in the directory.**

This is the file you will print.

● **Select file** Speech **and tap** [RETURN]. **Swap disks if prompted.**

File Speech should now be visible on the Review/Add/Change screen. Before you can print any AppleWorks file, it must be visible on this screen. Now you can print it.

Special Instructions for Printing   You may have special instructions for using a printer with AppleWorks. If so follow those instructions instead of the ones below.

● **Use these steps to get your printer ready:**

▲ **Be sure the printer has paper in it.**

▲ **If the printer is not on, switch it on now.**

▲ **If the Select light is off, tap the button next to it. (This light is some-times labeled SEL or On Line.)**

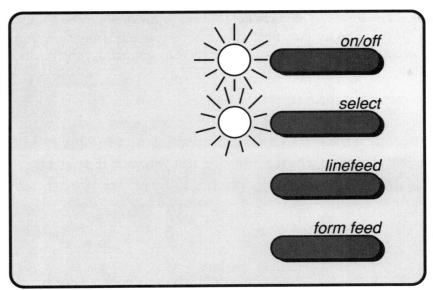

Control lights and buttons found on most printers. The select light must be on before printing can begin.

● **Use the following steps to make a printed copy of file Speech:**

▲ **Make sure your file is visible on the Review/Add/Change screen.**

▲ **Give the Print command ⌘P.**

▲ **If necessary follow the instructions for swapping disks and then tap (RETURN).**

▲ **Tap (RETURN) to print the whole file from the beginning.**

▲ **Select the name of the printer you are using and then tap (RETURN).**

▲ **Tap (RETURN) to print one copy of the file.**

The printing should start immediately. If it doesn't, check the Select light. If it is off, switch it on.

When printing is over, the computer returns to the Review/Add/Change screen. (There is a line of dashes under the information you typed, but it will go away as soon as you insert or delete anything in the file. The line isn't really part of the file; it just shows the end of a printed page.)

● **Use these steps to remove the printed copy from the printer:**

▲ **Tap the Select button on your printer again. The Select light should be off.**

▲ **Tap the Form Feed button. (This button may be labeled FF or TOF.)**

▲ **Carefully tear the paper off at a perforation.**

▲ **Tap the Select button on your printer once more.**

As you see, there are many steps in the process of making a printed copy of a word processor file. The to remember is how to get started: what screen to be at and what command to give. Once you are on the right track most of the other details follow.

Quick Check

1?   At which screen must you be to print a file?

_____

2?   What keyboard command tells the computer that you want to print a file?

_____

A Large File

Now for a new topic. So far you have worked with only a very small word processor file. No special tools are needed to move the cursor when the whole file is visible on the screen. Large word processor files are another matter.

Follow the Steps

● **If file Speech is still on the Review/Add/Change screen, tap** (ESC) **to go to the Main Menu. Then use the** Remove files... **command to erase Speech from memory. Throw out the changes to the file.**

● **Give the** Add Files... **command from the Main Menu. Then choose** The current disk **on the Add Files menu. Swap disks if prompted.**

The Data disk directory should now be visible on the screen. Notice the size of the files. Most are 1K in length. This means that they each contain 1024 characters at most. File Dickens, however, is a 7K file. This is the one you'll explore now.

● **Use the** (↓) **key to select** Dickens. **Then tap** (RETURN).

● **If prompted follow instructions for swapping disks.**

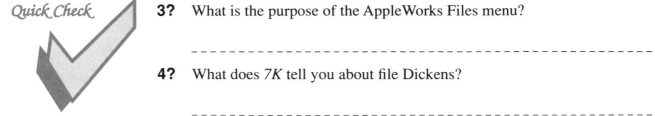

Quick Check

3?   What is the purpose of the AppleWorks Files menu?

_____

4?   What does *7K* tell you about file Dickens?

_____

Making Big Cursor Moves

You should now be at the Review/Add/Change screen. At the upper left you should see the file name Dickens. Your screen should look like this now:

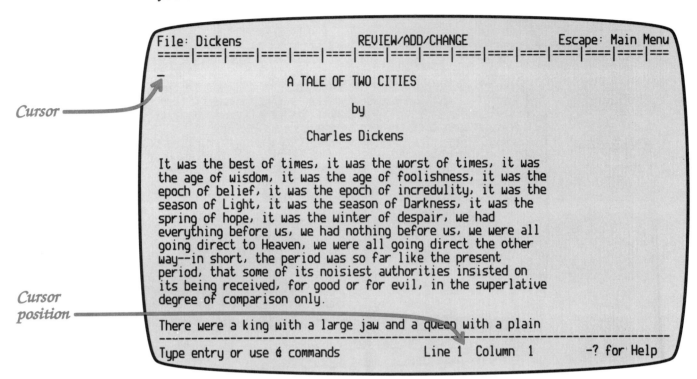

Cursor

Cursor position

The text of this file is too long to fit on one screen. In an earlier lab you learned to use the arrow keys to scroll back and forth through this file.

Follow the Steps

● **Hold down the ⬇ key to move the cursor to the end of the file.**

Information at the bottom of the screen shows that the cursor is at line 114, the last line of the file. You could use the ⬆ key in the same way to get back to the beginning of the file, but there is a faster way.

● **Hold down the ⌘ key and tap ①.**

The ⌘① command tells the computer to move the cursor to the beginning of the file.

● **Give the command ⌘⑨.**

The ⌘⑨ command tells the computer to move the cursor to the last text line in the file.

● **Give the command ⌘⑤.**

This command places the cursor at line 57, the middle line in the file. Your screen should look like this:

```
File: Dickens              REVIEW/ADD/CHANGE          Escape: Main Menu
=====|====|====|====|====|====|====|====|====|====|====|====|====|====|===
achievements as sentencing a youth to have his hands cut
off, his tongue torn out with pincers, and his body burned
alive, because he had not kneeled down in the rain to do
honour to a dirty procession of monks which passed within
his view, at a distance of some fifty or sixty yards.  It is
likely enough that, rooted in the woods of France and
Norway, there were growing trees, when that sufferer was put
to death, already marked by the Woodman, Fate, to come down
and be sawn into boards, to make a certain movable framework
with a sack and a knife in it, terrible in history.  It is
likely enouygh that in the rough outhouses of some tillers of
the heavy lands adjacent to Paris, there were sheltered from
the weather that very day, rude carts, bespattered with
rustic mire, snuffed about by pigs, and roosted in by
poultry, which the Farmer, Death, had already set apart to
be his tumbrils of the Revolution.  But that Woodman and
that Farmer, though they work unceasingly, work silently,
and no one heard them as they went about with muffled tread:
the rather, forasmuch as to entertain any suspicion that
they were awake, was to be atheistical and traitorous.
---------------------------------------------------------------------
Type entry or use ⌘ commands          Line 57  Column  1      -? for Help
```

Middle line ⟶

You can use other number keys with ⌘ to move quickly to other parts of the file. There is another way to move the cursor rapidly through the file.

● **Give the ⌘① command to move the cursor to the beginning of the file.**

● **Give the command ⌘↓.**

This command moves the cursor to the bottom line of whatever text is on the screen.

● **Give the ⌘↓ command again.**

When the cursor is already on the bottom line of the screen, the ⌘↓ command has a different effect: It displays the next 20 lines (one full screen) of text.

● **Keep giving the ⌘↓ command until the cursor is at the end of the file.**

● **Give the command ⌘↑.**

As you might guess, the ⌘↑ command is the reverse of the ⌘↓ command. If the cursor is not at the top of the screen, the ⌘↑ command moves it there.

● **Give the (⌂↑) command again.**

  If the cursor is already at the top line on the screen, the (⌂↑) command moves the cursor 20 lines (one full screen) up in the file.

● **Keep using (⌂↑) until the cursor is at the beginning of the file.**

◆ **The Dickens file** The text in file Dickens is 114 lines long—nearly six times as much as you can see at one time on the computer screen. The arrow keys give you a simple way to move from letter to letter or line to line in the file. With only the arrow keys, however, it would take a long time to move from the beginning to the end of a big file.

◆ **Scrolling up and down** In AppleWorks holding a key down has the same effect as tapping the key again and again. One way to move down the lines of a file is to hold the (↓) key down. The cursor quickly goes to the bottom line on the screen. After that the cursor stays at the bottom of the screen, but the text in the file starts moving up. As each new line appears at the bottom, a line disappears at the top. The text "scrolls" up the screen—just as if it were written on a scroll of paper that someone was rolling up behind the screen.

Moving the cursor through a file is like reading information printed on a paper scroll.

◆ **Jumping to the beginning or end** Many times you want to jump quickly to the beginning or end of a file. The command (⌂1) puts the first 20 lines of the file on the screen. The command (⌂9) brings the end of the file into view.

◆ **Other jumps**   The command ⌘5 brings the middle of the file into view. The computer puts the cursor at the beginning of the middle line of the file. Other number keys used with the ⌘ key cause jumps to other lines. Think of the file as being divided into eight equal parts. The ⌘1 command moves the cursor to the top line of the first part; ⌘2 moves it to the top line of the second part; ⌘3 moves it to the top line of the third part; and so on.

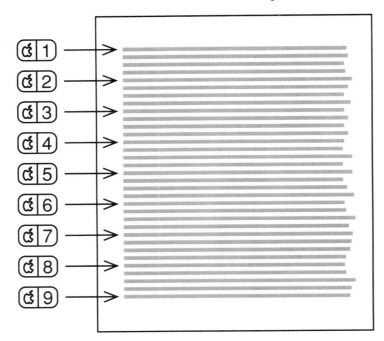

AppleWorks files are divided into eight equal parts. You can jump quickly to any part.

◆ **Moving by screens**   The AppleWorks Review/Add/Change screen shows 20 lines of a word processor file at a time. The command ⌘↓ allows you to move through the file one full screen at a time. If the cursor is not already at the bottom screen line, this command will put it there. After that each ⌘↓ brings another 20 lines of the file into view. In this way you can quickly go through an entire file without missing any lines. The ⌘↑ command allows you to move backward through the file in the same way.

Quick Check

5?   What single command moves the cursor to the beginning of the file? To the end of the file?

- -

6?   What does the ⌘↓ command do if the cursor is in the middle of the screen?

- -

7?   What does the ⌘↓ command do if the cursor is at the bottom of the screen?

- -

Moving the Cursor a Word at a Time

You've seen how to move up and down through a file quickly. You can also move the cursor left and right quickly.

Follow the Steps

- **Move the cursor to the beginning of line 8.**

- **Tap ⊟ until the cursor is at the beginning of the word** best.

  The cursor moves a character at a time, but there is a faster way.

- **Watch the screen as you give the command (⌑→).**

  This command moves the cursor forward one whole word at a time.

- **Give the (⌑→) command about 15 times.**

  Each time you give this command, the cursor moves forward one word. At the end of a line, the command moves the cursor to the first word on the next line.

- **Give the (⌑←) command a few times.**

  That moves the cursor back one word at a time. The (⌑) commands with arrow keys let you move the cursor rapidly through the file. You can move left or right one word at a time. You can move up or down one screen at a time.

- ◆ **Open-apple arrow keys**   You can think of the (⌑) key as a magnifier for the arrow keys. The (↑) key moves the cursor up one line. The (⌑↑) command moves the cursor up many lines. The (⌑) key has a similar effect on the left and right arrow keys. The command (⌑→) moves the cursor to the beginning of the next word in the file; (⌑←) moves to the beginning of the previous word. Holding down both (⌑) and (→) is like giving the (⌑→) command again and again. This is a handy way to move the cursor quickly through a sentence or paragraph.

- ◆ **Summary of cursor commands**   You have explored many different ways to move the cursor through a word processor file. The table below lists all the AppleWorks commands for moving the cursor and explains briefly what each one does.

Cursor Command	*Effect*
⊟, ⊟	Move left or right one space
⊡, ⊡	Move up or down one line
(⌑←), (⌑→)	Move left or right one word
(⌑↑), (⌑↓)	Move to the top or bottom screen line; if there, move up or down a full screen
(⌑1) through (⌑9)	Move proportional distances in file

Quick Check

8?   What does the ⌔→ command do?

- -

9?   What is the difference between using an arrow key by itself and using the same arrow key with the ⌔ key?

- -

That completes all the regular activities in this lab. If you have time, carry out some of the On Your Own activities below. When you finish, quit AppleWorks and remove the disks.

On Your Own

■ Load file KnockKnock into memory. Use it to practice printing.

■ Practice cursor moves on any of the word processor files on the Data disk.

Review Questions

1.   If you are at the Review/Add/Change screen, what does the ⌔P command tell the computer to do?

- -

2.   What AppleWorks screen allows you to edit a file?

- -

3.   How many lines of a long word processor file are visible at one time when you are editing the file?

- -

4.   What does *scrolling* mean?

- -

5.   What command moves the cursor down through a file, one full screen at a time?

- -

6.   What command moves the cursor to the last line of a file?

- -

7.   What command moves the cursor to the beginning of the next word in a word processor file?

- -

★

Goals

✔ Use keyboard commands to find pieces of text in a word processor file.
✔ Use keyboard commands to replace old text with new text.
✔ Be aware of problems that can arise when replacing text.

Finding Text

◆
★

Often you want to move the cursor to a word that you know is somewhere in the file but you don't know where. AppleWorks has a command to find text anywhere in a file.

Follow the Steps

● **Start the computer as usual with AppleWorks.**

● **Load file Dickens from your Computer Applications Data disk.**

● **Move the cursor to the beginning of the file.**

● **Give the Find command ⑤Ⓕ.**

The top line shows that you are at the Find screen. (As usual tapping ⒺⓈⒸ will undo the command.)

```
File: Dickens                    FIND        Escape: Review/Add/Change
=====|====|====|====|====|====|====|====|====|====|====|====|====|====|====|===

                         A TALE OF TWO CITIES

                                 by

                           Charles Dickens

        It was the best of times, it was the worst of times, it was
        the age of wisdom, it was the age of foolishness, it was the
        epoch of belief, it was the epoch of incredulity, it was the
        season of Light, it was the season of Darkness, it was the
        spring of hope, it was the winter of despair, we had
        everything before us, we had nothing before us, we were all
        going direct to Heaven, we were all going direct the other
        way--in short, the period was so far like the present
        period, that some of its noisiest authorities insisted on
        its being received, for good or for evil, in the superlative
        degree of comparison only.

        There were a king with a large jaw and a queen with a plain
        ------------------------------------------------------------------
Find? ▮Text▮ Page  Marker  Case sensitive text  Options for printer
```

60

The bottom line is prompting you for input. One of the five possible options is already selected.

● **Use the ⊖ and ⊖ keys to select each of the different options. Do *not* tap (RETURN) yet.**

There are five kinds of things you can find: Text, Page, Marker, Case sensitive text, and Options for printer. For now look for Text.

● **Select Text and tap (RETURN).**

The prompt at the bottom of the screen asks you to enter whatever text you want the computer to find.

● **Type king and tap (RETURN).**

The computer found the word king, scrolled to that part of the file, and highlighted the word.

```
File: Dickens                    FIND            Escape: Review/Add/Change
=====|====|====|====|====|====|====|====|====|====|====|====|====|====|====|===
epoch of belief, it was the epoch of incredulity, it was the
season of Light, it was the season of Darkness, it was the
spring of hope, it was the winter of despair, we had
everything before us, we had nothing before us, we were all
going direct to Heaven, we were all going direct the other
way--in short, the period was so far like the present
period, that some of its noisiest authorities insisted on
its being received, for good or for evil, in the superlative
degree of comparison only.

There were a king with a large jaw and a queen with a plain
face, on the throne of Engand; there were a king with a
large jaw and a queen with a fair face, on the throne of
France.  In both countries it was clearer than crystal to
the lords of the State preserves of loaves and fishes, that
things in general were settled forever.

It was the year of Our Lord one thousand seven hundred and
seventy-five.  Spiritual revelations were conceded to
England at that favoured period, as at this.  Mrs. Southcott
--------------------------------------------------------------------------
Find next occurrence?  No  Yes
```

"king" found

The prompt at the bottom of the screen asks whether you want to find the next occurrence of the word. No is already selected. If you found the word you are looking for, you can quit by tapping either (RETURN) or (N). If you are looking for another occurrence of the word, tap (Y).

● **Tap (Y) to find the next occurrence of king.**

This is the second occurrence of the word.

● **Tap (Y) again.**

As you see, the computer found king again, but this time it is a part of another word. The important point to remember is that the computer searches for a series of letters. It highlights that series whenever it finds it, whether as a separate word, a part of a word, or a whole group of words.

● **Tap Ⓨ again.**

This time, the computer found king inside the word taking.

● **Tap Ⓨ once more.**

The beep and the prompt at the bottom of the screen tell you that the computer didn't find any more occurrences. Try looking for another word.

● **As directed, tap the spacebar to get back to the Review/Add/Change screen.**

● **Move the cursor to the beginning of the file. Give the ⒹⒻ command, select** Text, **and tap** ⒭⒠⒯⒰⒭⒩.

The computer remembers the last word you wanted to find. (When you use the Text option, the computer treats KING, king and KiNg as the same.) If you wanted to look for king again, you would just tap ⒭⒠⒯⒰⒭⒩. To look for a different word, say queen, you must first delete the word already there.

● **Give the Yank command ⒹⓎ.**

Notice that KING has disappeared. The Yank command tells the computer to "yank out" all characters from the cursor to the end of the text entry line.

● **Type** queen **and tap** ⒭⒠⒯⒰⒭⒩.

● **Tap Ⓨ to find the next occurrence.**

The computer found the word queen once more.

● **Tap Ⓝ to stop the search.**

Nearly all word processor programs have a command for finding text and bringing it into view. This command is often called the **search** command. In AppleWorks the search command is the Find or ⒹⒻ command. Here are the steps you used to find the word king:

1. Move the cursor to the beginning of the file.

2. Give the Find command ⒹⒻ.

3. Select the Text option and tap ⒭⒠⒯⒰⒭⒩.

4. Enter the word to be found (king). You may have to erase a word or phrase already there before entering your word.

5. The computer finds the word and shows the part of the file containing it. If you want to find the next occurrence of the word, tap Ⓨ. Otherwise, tap Ⓝ.

You really only have to remember the first two steps. After that the computer prompts you for more information as it is needed.

◆ **Finding parts of words**   When you asked the computer to search for king it found the word twice, but it also found the same four letters as parts of the words making and taking. The computer looks for any match it can find between the text you type and the text in the file. (Some word processor programs let you limit the search to complete words.)

◆ **Case sensitive text**   Sometimes you want to find a word whether it is capitalized or not. At other times capitalization matters. Like most other word processor programs, AppleWorks lets you say what kind of search you want. If you select Text at step 3 above, the computer ignores capitalization. If you select Case sensitive text, the computer pays attention to capitalization. In other words the computer is sensitive to whether each letter is an uppercase or a lowercase letter. The table below shows examples.

Search for:	*In:*	*Text*	*Case Sensitive Text*
cat	cattle	match	match
cat	Cattle	match	no match
Cat	Cattle	match	match
Cat	cattle	match	no match

◆ **Erasing the previous selection**   If you use the ⌘F command a second time, the computer remembers the last word or phrase you were looking for. When the time comes for you to enter new text, you must first erase the old text. The simplest way to do this is to use the Yank command ⌘Y. It tells the computer to erase all text from the cursor to the end of the entry.

Quick Check

1?   What command tells the computer to search a file for a word or phrase that you type on the keyboard?

- -

2?   What command erases characters from the cursor to the end of the line?

- -

Finding and Replacing Text

◆
★
Quite often the reason you want to find a phrase is to change it. Appleworks has a single command for finding one piece of text and replacing it with new text.

Here is an example. The Dickens passage uses British spelling for English words. American spelling is usually the same but not always. For example, Dickens uses the words *honour, favour, gaol,* and *recognise* where an

American would write *honor, favor, jail,* and *recognize*. You can use the word processor program to change the spellings from British style to American style. Begin by changing the words that end in *our*.

Follow the Steps

- **Move the cursor to the beginning of the file.**
- **Give the Replace command ⌘R.**

The new Replace screen is similar to the Find screen, except that there are fewer options listed at the bottom.

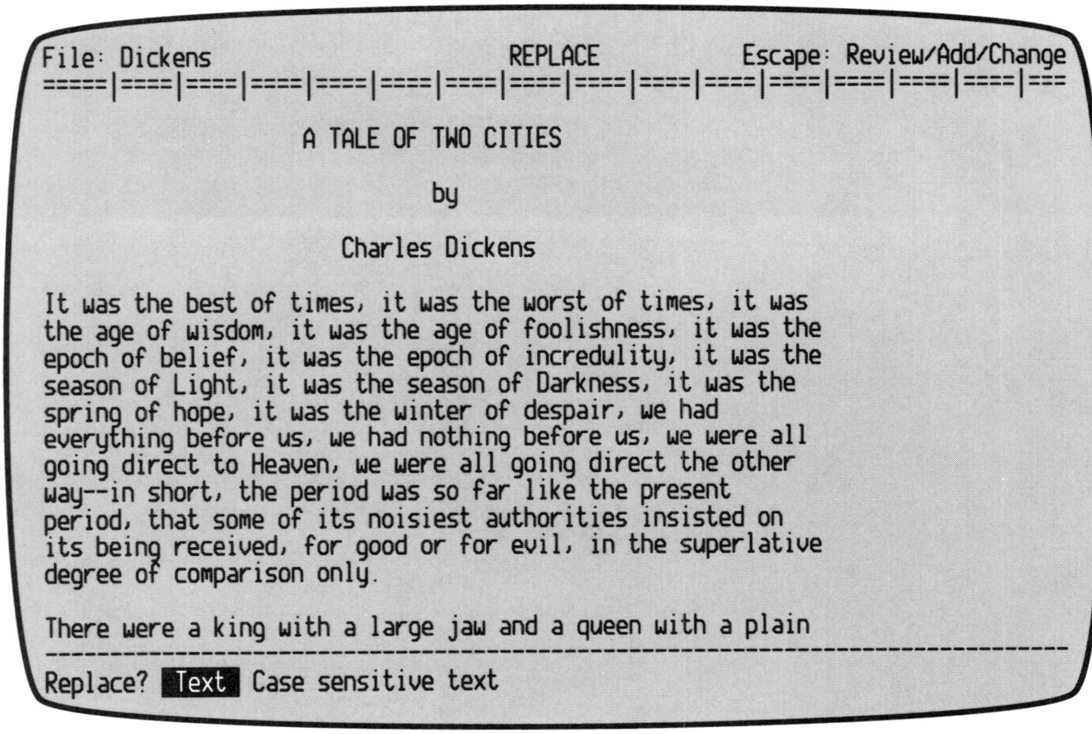
File: Dickens REPLACE Escape: Review/Add/Change
A TALE OF TWO CITIES
by
Charles Dickens
It was the best of times, it was the worst of times, it was the age of wisdom, it was the age of foolishness, it was the epoch of belief, it was the epoch of incredulity, it was the season of Light, it was the season of Darkness, it was the spring of hope, it was the winter of despair, we had everything before us, we had nothing before us, we were all going direct to Heaven, we were all going direct the other way--in short, the period was so far like the present period, that some of its noisiest authorities insisted on its being received, for good or for evil, in the superlative degree of comparison only.
There were a king with a large jaw and a queen with a plain
Replace? Text Case sensitive text

In this mode, the computer will look for only two things: `Text` or `Case sensitive text`. **Case sensitive** means that the computer should treat capital and lowercase versions of the same letter as different characters. For example, *Honour* and *honour* are treated differently. In `Text` mode, however, capitalization is ignored when searching for a word or phrase.

- **Select** `Case sensitive text` **and tap RETURN.**

This is the safest choice when replacing text, since you usually don't want to replace a capitalized word with one that is not capitalized.

The prompt at the bottom of the screen is asking for the text that you want the computer to find. If there is text there already, you should erase it.

- **Give the Yank command ⌘Y to erase** `QUEEN`**.**
- **Type the letters** `our` **and tap RETURN.**

The new prompt asks for the replacement text.

● **Type the letters** or **and tap** (RETURN).

The next prompt asks whether you want to replace the words one at a time or all the words in the file at the same time. It's safer to replace words one at a time. That allows you to check each change before the computer makes it.

● **Select** One at a time **and tap** (RETURN).

As you see, the computer found our in the word favoured.

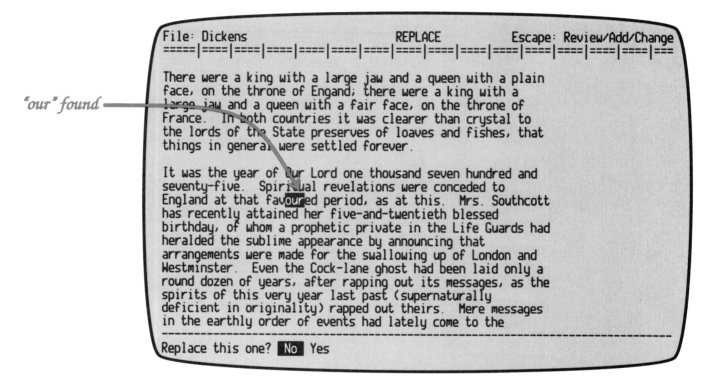

"our" found

```
File: Dickens                      REPLACE          Escape: Review/Add/Change
=====|====|====|====|====|====|====|====|====|====|====|====|====|====|===

There were a king with a large jaw and a queen with a plain
face, on the throne of Engand; there were a king with a
large jaw and a queen with a fair face, on the throne of
France.  In both countries it was clearer than crystal to
the lords of the State preserves of loaves and fishes, that
things in general were settled forever.

It was the year of Our Lord one thousand seven hundred and
seventy-five.  Spiritual revelations were conceded to
England at that favoured period, as at this.  Mrs. Southcott
has recently attained her five-and-twentieth blessed
birthday, of whom a prophetic private in the Life Guards had
heralded the sublime appearance by announcing that
arrangements were made for the swallowing up of London and
Westminster.  Even the Cock-lane ghost had been laid only a
round dozen of years, after rapping out its messages, as the
spirits of this very year last past (supernaturally
deficient in originality) rapped out theirs.  Mere messages
in the earthly order of events had lately come to the
-----------------------------------------------------------------------
Replace this one?  No  Yes
```

The prompt asks whether you want to replace this or not.

● **Tap** (Y).

Now the old spelling is gone. The new spelling has replaced it. The next step is to see whether there are any more occurrences of our in the file.

● **Tap** (Y) **to find the next occurrence.**

The computer finds our in favoured.

● **Tap** (Y) **to make the change.**

Again you have replaced the old spelling with the new one.

● **Tap** (Y) **to find the next word containing** our.

Now the computer finds our in honour.

● **Tap** (Y) **to replace and tap** (Y) **again to find the next occurrence.**

This time the computer finds our in four. You do not want the spelling changed here.

● **Tap Ⓝ or ⟨RETURN⟩ to avoid making the change.**

Now you can see why it was a good idea to make the changes one at a time and check each change before it is made.

● **Continue the process until no more *our* words are found. Then tap the spacebar to get back to the Review/Add/Change screen.**

That completes the replacement process. You can use the same process to change the British spelling of *recognise* to the American spelling *recognize*.

● **Move the cursor to the beginning of the file.**

The cursor must be at the beginning of the file if you want to search the whole file.

● **Use the ⌘R command to replace** ise **with** ize, **one at a time.**

You should have found only one occurrence of the British spelling.

● **Tap the spacebar to go back to the Review/Add/Change screen.**

● **Use the same method to replace** gaol **with** jail.

◆ **Replacing text**   Most word processor programs have a powerful (and sometimes dangerous) command called **search and replace**. The AppleWorks command is ⌘R. Suppose that you have written a report on Buffalo Bill. Later you discover that you misspelled his name as *Bufalo*. Here is how to use the AppleWorks search-and-replace command to fix all the misspellings in the whole file:

1. Move the cursor to the beginning of the file.

2. Give the Replace command ⌘R.

3. Choose Case sensitive text and tap ⟨RETURN⟩.

4. Enter the word you want to find (Bufalo).

5. Enter the word you want to replace it with (Buffalo).

6. Select All (not One at a time) and tap ⟨RETURN⟩.

Again the important things to remember are the first two steps. The computer prompts you after that. As soon as you carry out the last step, the computer begins searching the file. Whenever it finds the old text, it replaces it with the new text and then goes ahead with the search.

◆ **Using abbreviations**   The search-and-replace command can make life easy when you are writing a paper that contains the same phrase again and again. For example, if you were writing about the United States and the Soviet Union, you could just type US and SU as quick abbreviations. When the paper was finished, you could use the search-and-replace command to change US to United States everywhere. Then you could change SU to Soviet Union.

Quick Check

3? What AppleWorks command substitutes one phrase for another in a word processor file?

_ _

4? What does *case sensitive* mean?

_ _

How Things Can Go Wrong

As we said earlier, it is possible to have the computer make all the replacements without asking you about each one. This is a powerful command, but you have to be very careful when you use it. Here is an example of how things can go wrong:

Follow the Steps

● **Move the cursor to the beginning of the file.**

● **Give the ⌘R command. Select** Case sensitive text **and tap** (RETURN).

● **At the prompt, erase** gaol, **type** we, **and tap** (RETURN).

● **At the next prompt, erase** jail, **type** all of us, **and tap** (RETURN).

The computer is now ready to replace we with all of us.

● **At the final prompt, select** All **and tap** (RETURN).

It takes a little time to replace all occurrences of we with all of us. When the job is done, your screen looks like this:

Replacement

```
File: Dickens            REVIEW/ADD/CHANGE         Escape: Main Menu
=====|=====|=====|=====|=====|=====|=====|=====|=====|=====|=====|=====|=====|===
three dead, and then got shot dead himself by the other
four, "in consequence of the failure of his ammunition:"
after which the mail was robbed in peace; that magnificent
potentate, the Lord Mayor of London, was made to stand and
deliver on Turnham Greene, by one highwayman, who despoiled
the illustrious creature in sight of all his retinue;
prisoners in London jails fought battles with their
turnkeys, and the majesty of the law fired blunderbusses in
among them, loaded with rounds of shot and ball; thieves
snipped off diamond crosses from the necks of noble lords at
Court drawing-rooms; musketeers all of usnt into St.
Giles's, to search for contraband goods, and the mob fired
on the musketeers, and the musketeers fired on the mob, and
nobody thought any of these occurrences much out of the
common way.  In the midst of them, the hangman, ever busy
and ever worse than useless, was in constant requisition;
now, stringing up long rows of miscellaneous criminals; now,
hanging a house breaker on Saturday who had been taken on
Tuesday; now, burning people in the hand at Newgate by the
dozen, and now burning pamphlets at the door of Westminster
---------------------------------------------------------------------
Type entry or use ⌘ commands Line 93 Column 42 -?  for Help
```

Notice that the computer places the cursor just right of the final replacement. The text reads `musketeers all of usnt into St. Giles's`. Something went wrong. Can you see why?

● **Look at the end of line 69.**

The text reads `they all of usre awake`. You probably see the problem. You told the computer to replace `we` by `all of us` wherever `we` appeared. So the computer changed `went` to `all of usnt` and it changed `were` to `all of usre`.

Suppose you make a serious mistake while using the Replace command. What can be done? One solution is to work your way through the file and repair all the damage. Sometimes, however, it is easier to throw away all your changes and begin with a fresh copy of the file. Here is how to do that.

● **Go back to the Main Menu. Give the** `Remove files...` **command.**

● **If necessary select** `Dickens` **and then tap** (RETURN).

● **Give the command** `Throw out the changes to the file.`

● **Tap** (Y) **to tell the computer you really do want to throw away the file containing the changes.**

At this point, the copy of Dickens that was in memory is gone. However, the original version is still on your Computer Applications Data disk. If you wanted to make further changes, you could move a fresh copy of the file into memory.

◆ **Playing it safe**   To avoid accidents when searching and replacing text, select the `One at a time` option instead of the `All` option. The computer will then stop and ask whether you want each change made. If you say yes, the computer makes the change; if you say no, the change is not made.

◆ **Disaster time**   No matter how careful you are while editing, sooner or later you will make a mistake. In trying to fix the first error, you may find things getting worse and worse. What should you do? Probably the best course is to erase the version of the file in the computer's memory. (In AppleWorks terms, remove it from the Desktop.) Then load back into memory the last version you saved on your disk.

◆ **Strong advice**   What if you have not saved a copy on your disk? Then you are out of luck. You have much typing and editing ahead. You can be ready for such disasters if you follow this simple advice: Every ten minutes or so, use the (ᏪS) command to save your work on the disk. If disaster strikes later, you will have lost only a few minutes of work.

Quick Check

5?   What is the safest way to replace one word with another everywhere in the file?

6?   Suppose you make several mistakes while replacing text in a word processor file. The file is getting further and further from what you intended. What is usually the best thing to do?

That brings you to the end the regular lab activities. If you have time, do some of the On Your Own activities. Then quit the computer in the usual way.

On Your Own

■   Clear the Desktop. Put file BadIE on the Desktop. The words in this file don't follow the "*i* before *e*" spelling rule. Use the Replace command to change ei to ie as needed. Use the Replace command again to change ie to ei as needed. Use the ⌘N command to change the file name to GoodIE; then save it.

■   Put file Dickens back on the Desktop. Practice cursor moves. Practice finding words and phrases. Practice replacing words. Discard changes to the file when you are finished.

Review Questions

1.   Suppose you want to find the first occurrence of *king* in a file. What are the first two things you should do?

----

2.   Suppose you want replace *king* with *ruler* everywhere in a word processor file. What are the first two things you should do?

----

3.   Suppose you want to find the first occurrence of *Queen* in a file, but you do not want the computer to find *queen*. When prompted, which option should you choose: Text or Case sensitive text?

----

4.   Sometimes the search-and-replace command is called "search-and-destroy." Why might someone say that?

----

5.   What is the safest way to replace one word with another word everywhere in a file?

Goals

✔ Delete a text block from a word processor file.
✔ Move a text block within a word processor file.
✔ Save a Desktop file with a new name.

Deleting a Text Block

So far in this chapter you have edited word processor files by inserting and deleting words, one character at a time. In this lab you will begin learning how to work with **text blocks**. A text block can be a single character, a whole word, several lines, or several paragraphs, for example.

Follow the Steps

● **Start the computer with AppleWorks as usual.**

● **Move a copy of file Dickens from your Computer Applications Data disk into memory.**

Of the three block-editing commands in AppleWorks, the Delete command is the simplest. You will use file Dickens to see how this command works. Here is how to delete the first paragraph and the blank line after it.

● **Use the arrow keys to move the cursor to line 8, column 1.**

This places the cursor at the beginning of the first paragraph.

● **Give the Delete command ⌒D.**

This command changes the name of the screen to Delete Text. The letter I at the beginning of the paragraph is now highlighted. This tells you where the cursor was when you gave the Delete command. This place is the starting point for the deletion. The prompt at the bottom of the screen asks you to highlight the text block you want to delete. (The **blobs**—the checkerboard patterns—show where the (RETURN) key was tapped when this file was created.) Here's how to highlight the whole paragraph.

● **Tap the (↓) key.**

That highlights the first line and the first character on the next line.

● **Tap the (↓) key until you have highlighted the entire paragraph and the blank line after it.**

You have now selected the entire block of text to be deleted. The figure on the next page shows how your screen should look.

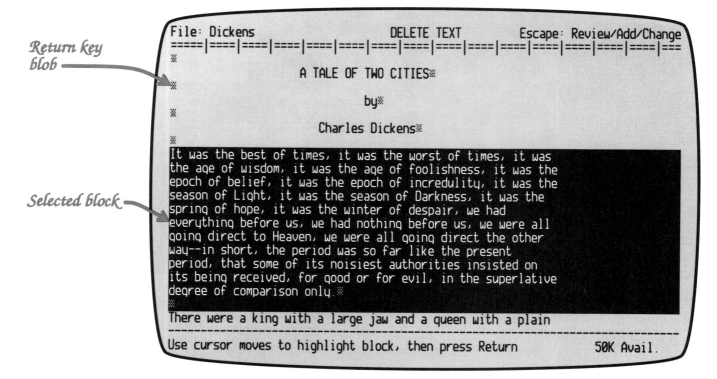

Return key blob

Selected block

File: Dickens   DELETE TEXT   Escape: Review/Add/Change
=====|====|====|====|====|====|====|====|====|====|====|====|====|====|====|===
※
                          A TALE OF TWO CITIES※

                                  by※

                           Charles Dickens※
※
It was the best of times, it was the worst of times, it was
the age of wisdom, it was the age of foolishness, it was the
epoch of belief, it was the epoch of incredulity, it was the
season of Light, it was the season of Darkness, it was the
spring of hope, it was the winter of despair, we had
everything before us, we had nothing before us, we were all
going direct to Heaven, we were all going direct the other
way--in short, the period was so far like the present
period, that some of its noisiest authorities insisted on
its being received, for good or for evil, in the superlative
degree of comparison only.※

There were a king with a large jaw and a queen with a plain

Use cursor moves to highlight block, then press Return   50K Avail.

● **Tap (RETURN) to delete the block.**

The selected block is no longer in the file in memory. Once deleted there is no way to get the block back except by reentering it at the keyboard or by reloading the original file from the disk. *Be very careful when you use the Delete command.*

As you have seen, deleting a text block begins with selecting and highlighting it. Explore the selection process some more.

● **Move the cursor to line 11, column 10.**

● **Give the Delete command ⌘D.**

Once more the computer is waiting for you to select a block of text.

● **Hold the → key down for a few seconds.**

That selects characters to the right of the starting point.

● **Tap the ← key a few times.**

You can undo a selection by using the arrow keys.

● **Tap the ← key until the only letter highlighted is the starting point.**

● **Tap the ← key a few more times.**

That selects characters to the left of the starting point. The starting point is always at the beginning or the end of whatever block of text you select.

● **See what happens when you hold down each of the arrow keys for a few seconds.**

The arrow keys allow you to select any block of text that either begins with or ends at the starting point.

● **Give the ⌐1 command.**

As you see, this selects the block between the starting point and the beginning of the file.

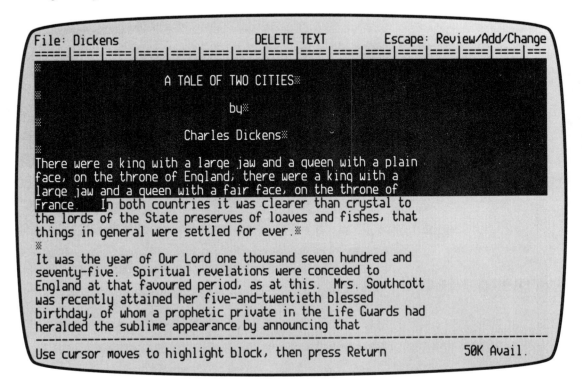

```
File: Dickens                    DELETE TEXT          Escape: Review/Add/Change
=====|====|====|====|====|====|====|====|====|====|====|====|====|====|====|===

                        A TALE OF TWO CITIES

                                by

                           Charles Dickens

There were a king with a large jaw and a queen with a plain
face, on the throne of England; there were a king with a
large jaw and a queen with a fair face, on the throne of
France.   In both countries it was clearer than crystal to
the lords of the State preserves of loaves and fishes, that
things in general were settled for ever.

It was the year of Our Lord one thousand seven hundred and
seventy-five.  Spiritual revelations were conceded to
England at that favoured period, as at this.  Mrs. Southcott
was recently attained her five-and-twentieth blessed
birthday, of whom a prophetic private in the Life Guards had
heralded the sublime appearance by announcing that
-----------------------------------------------------------------------------
Use cursor moves to highlight block, then press Return          50K Avail.
```

Any of the commands you have used to move the cursor can also be used to select text for deletion. For example, the ⌐9 command would select all text from the starting point to the end of the file.

● **Give the ⌐9 command. Then tap RETURN.**

That deleted most of the file. You can use this feature to delete all the text in a file if you choose.

◆ **Block editing**   You can edit any word processor file by inserting or deleting text one character at a time, but some tasks go slowly working this way. To speed things up most word processors have specialized tools for working with whole blocks of text.

◆ **Deleting a block**   The simplest block-editing tool in AppleWorks is the Delete command ⌐D. To use it move the cursor to the first (or last) character of the block of text you want to delete. Next type ⌐D. When prompted use any cursor-moving commands to select the block of text you wish to delete. As you select the text, the computer highlights it on the screen. After you select the block, tap RETURN to delete it.

◆ **A warning**   If you change your mind before tapping (RETURN), you can "back out" of the Delete command by tapping (ESC). Once you tap (RETURN), however, the text is removed from the copy of the file in memory. There are only two ways to get it back: retype it (if you remember what it was) or get a fresh copy of the file from your disk. This is another reason to save a copy of the file you are working on every few minutes.

Quick Check

1?   Suppose you want to delete a block of text from a file. Where should the cursor be when you give the Delete command?

_____

2?   After giving the Delete command, how do you tell the computer which text block you want deleted?

_____

3?   How would you use the Delete command to erase all the text in a file in memory?

_____

Moving a Text Block

◆
★

Sometimes instead of deleting a block of text, you simply want to move the block from one place to another in a file. The AppleWorks Move command does the job.

Follow the Steps

● **Use the** `Remove files...` **command on the Main Menu to clear the Desktop. Throw out the changes to the file.**

● **Load file MixedUp from your Data disk. (Swap disks if prompted.)**

● **Read the paragraph. Think about how it could be improved.**

You probably had trouble following what the writer had in mind. The basic facts are right, but the sentences don't go together well. Here are the same sentences rearranged so the paragraph makes more sense.

```
In AppleWorks, "the Desktop" stands for the computer's
memory unit. The files that you make, or load from a disk,
go on the Desktop. You can have up to 12 files on the
Desktop at the same time. However, the information on the
computer's Desktop is not permanent. Everything disappears
when you switch off the power. When you are finished with a
Desktop file, you should save it permanently on your disk.
Saving a computer file is like putting an office file back
in a file cabinet.
```

Your task is to move the sentences in file MixedUp so that the paragraph looks like the one above. To do this you will use a new AppleWorks command for moving a block of text.

● **Read the third sentence on your screen.**

This is the topic sentence and should come first. Here's how to move the sentence to the beginning of the paragraph.

● **Move the cursor under the letter I at the beginning of the third sentence.**

This will be the starting point for the text block to be moved.

● **Give the Move command Ⓒ︎Ⓜ︎.**

This command changes the name of the screen to Move Text. At the bottom of the screen, you see a new prompt and three options. (You will learn about the clipboard option later.)

● **Give the Within document command by tapping ⟨RETURN⟩.**

As with the Delete command, your next task is to select the block of text to be moved.

● **Use the arrow keys to highlight the third sentence, including the period and the two spaces after it.**

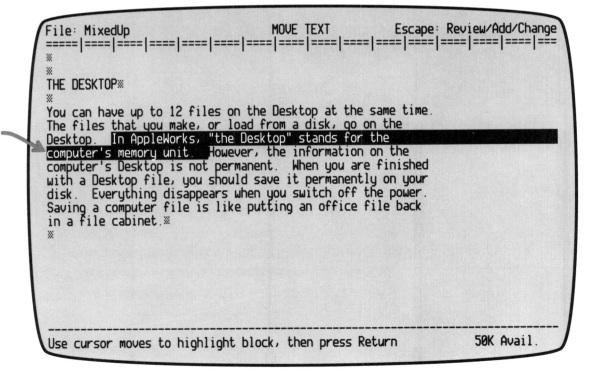

Block to move

```
File: MixedUp                    MOVE TEXT          Escape: Review/Add/Change
=====|====|====|====|====|====|====|====|====|====|====|====|====|====|===
 ※
 ※
THE DESKTOP※
 ※
You can have up to 12 files on the Desktop at the same time.
The files that you make, or load from a disk, go on the
Desktop.  In AppleWorks, "the Desktop" stands for the
computer's memory unit.  However, the information on the
computer's Desktop is not permanent.  When you are finished
with a Desktop file, you should save it permanently on your
disk.  Everything disappears when you switch off the power.
Saving a computer file is like putting an office file back
in a file cabinet.※
 ※



-----------------------------------------------------------------------
Use cursor moves to highlight block, then press Return        50K Avail.
```

Here's how to move the selected block to the beginning of the paragraph.

● **Tap** (RETURN).

The sentence is still highlighted, but there is a new prompt.

● **Use the arrow keys to move the cursor under the** Y **at the beginning of the paragraph. Then tap** (RETURN).

That did it. The computer moved the selected block to the new cursor location. That completes the first change. Now take a moment to read the paragraph again. The second and third sentences are still out of order. Move the second sentence so it follows the third.

● **Put the cursor under the** Y **at the beginning of the second sentence.**

● **Use the Move command and the arrow keys to select the whole sentence, including the period and spaces that follow it. Then tap** (RETURN).

● **Move the cursor under the** H **in** However.

This is where you want to move the highlighted sentence.

● **Tap** (RETURN).

As before, the computer moves the selected text to the new location. Almost done; two sentences are still out of order.

● **Use the Move command to move the sentence that begins with** When **after the sentence that begins with** Everything.

Now all the sentences are in proper order in the paragraph. You can use the Move command to move any selected text (words, phrases, sentences, paragraphs, etc.) to a new location in the file.

◆ **Moving a block**   The Move command (⌘M) works a lot like the Delete command. You first select the block of text you want moved and then tap (RETURN). The block remains highlighted. You next move the cursor to a new location and tap (RETURN). The computer moves the highlighted block to the new location.

Quick Check

4?   Where should the cursor be when you give the Move command?

_ _

5?   After you have selected the text block to be moved and have tapped (RETURN), what else must you do to move the block?

_ _

Saving a File with a Different Name

Earlier you loaded file MixedUp into memory. Then you used the Move command to change the order of sentences in the file. Suppose you now want to save the new version of the file on your disk, but *not* to erase the old version. You can do this by changing the name of the file in memory before saving it. AppleWorks has a command for changing the name of a file in memory. (You may have already used this command in On Your Own activities.)

Follow the Steps

● **With the new version of file MixedUp on the Review/Add/Change screen, give the Name command ⌒N. (If prompted swap disks and tap RETURN.)**

You are now at the Change Filename screen. The current name of the file in memory (MixedUp) is shown at both the top and the bottom of the screen. The prompt line asks you to enter a new name for the file. However, you must get rid of the old name first.

● **Give the Yank command ⌒Y.**

That erases the file name in the prompt line. The flashing cursor means that the computer is waiting for you to enter the new file name.

● **Type FixedUp and tap RETURN. Note the file name at the upper left corner of the screen.**

That does it. The file in memory is now named FixedUp and you can save it on your Data disk without erasing file MixedUp.

● **Give the Save command ⌒S. (If prompted swap disks and tap RETURN.)**

The edited file FixedUp is now saved on your Data disk. The original file MixedUp is also on the disk.

Quick Check

6? You have just loaded a file into memory and have used the Name command to change its name. Does that automatically change the file's name on the disk?

7? What screen must you be at to use the Save command ⌒S?

This brings you to the end of the regular activities. If you have time, do some of the On Your Own activities on the next page. Then quit AppleWorks in the usual way. Throw away any changes you do not want to keep.

On Your Own

■ Clear the Desktop. Load file Disorder into memory. This file needs to be put into alphabetical order. Use the Move command to alphabetize the list. Change the file name to Order and save it.

■ Load file KnockKnock into memory. Practice deleting jokes and moving jokes to new locations in the file. When you have finished, throw away the changes.

Review Questions

1. Using the Delete command is one way to delete a paragraph. What is another way?

   ----

2. If you want to delete a block of text, where must the cursor be when you give the Delete command?

   ----

3. Suppose you have given the Delete command. What keys or commands can you use to highlight the text block you want deleted?

   ----

4. Suppose the cursor is at the middle of a word processor file. You want to delete *all* the text in the file. What is the easiest way to do this?

   ----

5. Suppose you gave the Delete command and highlighted a block of text. Then you changed your mind and decided not to delete it. What should you do?

   ----

6. Suppose you want to move a sentence from one place to another in a word processor file. What are the first two things you should do?

Goals

✔ Make a duplicate copy of a text block in a word processor file.
✔ Use the clipboard to move text blocks from one file to another.

Copying a Text Block

In the previous lab you learned two commands for working with blocks of text. The Delete command erases a highlighted block of characters from a word processor file. The Move command moves a block of characters from one place in a file to another. Once in a while you may want to make a duplicate copy of a text block and put it someplace else in a file. AppleWorks has a command for doing this.

Follow the
Steps

● **Start the computer with AppleWorks as usual.**

● **Move a copy of file KnockKnock from your Data disk into memory.**

Your screen should look like this:

```
File: KnockKnock          REVIEW/ADD/CHANGE          Escape: Main Menu
=====|====|====|====|====|====|====|====|====|====|====|====|====|====|====|===

KNOCK-KNOCK JOKES

STANDARD FORM

     Knock, Knock!
          Who's there?
     xxx
          xxx who?
     xxx yyy

OUR FAVORITES

     Knock, Knock!
          Who's there?
     Sam and Janet
          Sam and Janet who?
     Sam and Janet evening, you will meet a stranger...



----------------------------------------------------------------------
Type entry or use ⌂ commands          Line 1  Column 1          -? for Help
```

● **Scroll through the file and read the jokes.**

Knock-knock jokes all have the same form. The top part of the file shows that form.

● **Give the ⌒1 command to go to the top of the file.**

In the standard form, xxx stands for the answer to the first question and yyy is the rest of the answer to the second question. If you wanted to add some knock-knock jokes to this file, you could use this standard form to save some typing. To do this you need to copy the form to other places in the file. The Copy command in AppleWorks does this.

● **Move the cursor down to the beginning of the blank line after** STANDARD FORM.

● **Give the Copy command ⌒C.**

The Copy Text screen is similar to the Move Text screen, which you saw earlier. The prompt line is exactly the same.

● **Tap RETURN to tell the computer you want to copy a block of text within file KnockKnock.**

As with the Move command, the computer is waiting for you to select the text block you want copied.

● **Use the arrow keys to highlight the standard form including the blank lines before and after the form. Then tap RETURN.**

The selected block remains highlighted. The prompt line tells you to move the cursor to the place where you want the copy to appear.

● **Give the ⌒9 command to move the cursor to the end of the file.**

● **Tap RETURN.**

There it is. The computer put a copy of the highlighted block at the cursor position.

● **Give the ⌒1 command to return to the beginning of the file.**

As you can see, the original block is still there. This is the difference between the Copy command and the Move command. The Copy command tells the computer to make a duplicate copy of a text block and put the copy elsewhere in the file. The Move command tells the computer to move the actual text block, not a copy.

● **Go to the end of the file.**

Now that you have a copy of the knock-knock form, you can edit it to add a new joke to the file. Here's one.

● **Move the cursor just above the first** xxx **in the new copy of the form.**

● **Give the Replace command ⌒R.**

● **Use the methods you learned in the last lab to replace all occurrences of xxx with** Izzy **in your new copy of the knock-knock form.**

Your screen should now look like this:

```
File: KnockKnock            REVIEW/ADD/CHANGE            Escape: Main Menu
=====|====|====|====|====|====|====|====|====|====|====|====|====|===
          Wendy who?
      Wendy wind blows, de cradle will rock...


YOUR FAVORITES

   Knock, Knock!
        Who's there?
   Izzy
        Izzy who?
   Izzy yyy




----------------------------------------------------------------------
Type entry or use ₡ commands           Line 55  Column 10      -? for Help
```

● **Finally, delete** yyy **and insert** come, Izzy go!.

Now you have a new joke in the file.

● **Use the Name command** ₡N **to change the name of the file to** MyJokes.

● **Use the Save command** ₡S **to save file MyJokes.**

You can use the Copy and Replace commands to add more jokes to file MyJokes.

◆ **Copying a block**   The Copy command ₡C works almost exactly like the Move command. You first select a text block and tap (RETURN). When you move the cursor and tap (RETURN), a copy of the highlighted block is inserted at the new location. The result is that you now have two identical text blocks at different places in the file.

1?   Where should the cursor be when you give the Copy command?

_____

2?   What is the difference in the effect of the Copy and the Move commands?

_____

How the Clipboard Works

◆
★

When the computer moves or copies a block of text within a file, a copy of the block is stored in a special part of memory. In AppleWorks this part of memory is called the **clipboard**. The clipboard has other uses, so you should have a clear picture of how it works.

◆ **A simple example**   An example will be helpful. Suppose a word processor file contains the following text:

It was the best of times. worst of times.

The goal is to edit the text so that it becomes

It was the best of times. It was the worst of times.

This can be done by making a copy of the block It was the and the space after it, and inserting the copy just before the word worst. The Apple-Works Copy command will do this job.

◆ **Copy command, first stage**   When copying text within the same file, the Copy command is carried out in two main stages. The figure below shows the first stage.

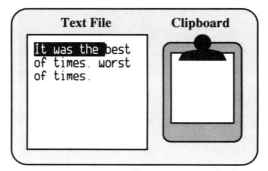
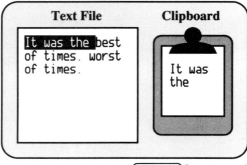

Copy command given,
Within document **chosen,**
text selected

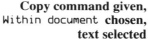

(RETURN) **key tapped**

In the first frame the Copy command has been given and the text block is selected. There is nothing on the clipboard now. In the second frame (RETURN) has been tapped. The copy is now in the clipboard area of memory. The text block in the file is still highlighted.

◆ **Copy command, second stage**   At the beginning of the second stage the clipboard contains the text to be copied. The figure below shows the second stage of the copy process.

Cursor moved | (RETURN) key tapped again

The first frame shows the cursor at the place where the copy will be inserted. The second frame shows the file and clipboard after (RETURN) is tapped. The text that was on the clipboard is now in the file. The clipboard area of memory is erased. As you can see, the clipboard stores information during the copy process and is empty afterward.

◆ **Move command, first stage**   Suppose that the Move command is used instead of the Copy command in this same example. As the figure below shows, the first stage of the Move command is exactly the same as the first stage of the Copy command.

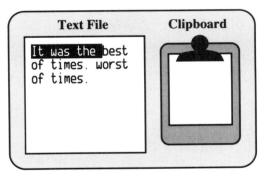

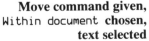

Move command given,
Within document **chosen,**
text selected | (RETURN) key tapped

◆ **Move command, second stage**   As before, the second stage begins with a copy of the selected block on the clipboard. The figure below shows what happens during the second stage.

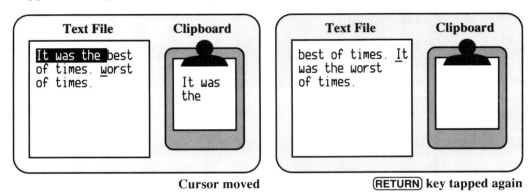

Cursor moved   (RETURN) **key tapped again**

The second frame shows the difference between this command and the Copy command. At the end of the Move process, the selected text is deleted from the file. Everything else is the same.

◆ **Role of the clipboard**   As these examples show, the role of the clipboard is the same for both the Copy and Move commands. In both cases a text block is copied onto the clipboard; then the block is copied back into the file at a different location; and then the clipboard is erased.

Quick Check

3?   In AppleWorks what is the clipboard?

4?   What commands put blocks of text on the clipboard?

Using the Clipboard to Move Text between Files

You now know all the tools needed to edit and move blocks of text within a file. Sometimes, however, you may want to move a block of text from one file to another. To do this, you must use the `To clipboard` and `From clipboard` options.

Follow the Steps

● **Go to the Main Menu and clear the Desktop.**

● **Load file Letter and read it. (If necessary swap disks as directed.)**

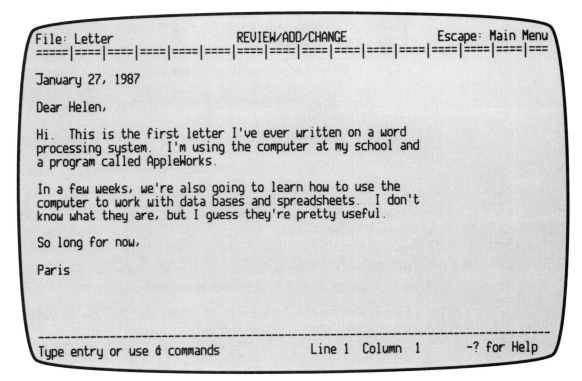

```
File: Letter                    REVIEW/ADD/CHANGE              Escape: Main Menu
=====|====|====|====|====|====|====|====|====|====|====|====|====|====|====|===

January 27, 1987

Dear Helen,

Hi.  This is the first letter I've ever written on a word
processing system.  I'm using the computer at my school and
a program called AppleWorks.

In a few weeks, we're also going to learn how to use the
computer to work with data bases and spreadsheets.  I don't
know what they are, but I guess they're pretty useful.

So long for now,

Paris


_____
Type entry or use ⌂ commands              Line 1  Column  1      -? for Help
```

Suppose you wrote a letter like this to a friend. Before sending it you decide to add one of your knock-knock jokes. You have a file full of jokes, so it would be nice to have the computer make a copy of one of your jokes and put it into your letter. Like many word processor programs, AppleWorks gives you a way to do this.

● **Go to the Main Menu and load file KnockKnock into memory.**

Now you have two files in memory. KnockKnock is visible on the Review/Add/Change screen, but file Letter is also in the computer's memory. You will return to it in a minute. For now you will select the knock-knock joke you want to copy into file Letter.

● **Scroll through the file and decide which joke you want to move.**

● **Place the cursor on the blank line just above your joke.**

● **Give the Copy command.**

You have seen the Copy Text screen before. This time, you do *not* want the block to stay within file KnockKnock. Instead, you want to put the copy in the clipboard area of memory.

● **Select** To clipboard... **and tap** (RETURN).

● **Use the arrow keys to select the rest of the joke and the blank line after it. Then tap** (RETURN).

You are now back at the Review/Add/Change screen for file Knock-Knock. Although you can't see it, the clipboard portion of memory now contains a copy of your joke. You no longer need file KnockKnock.

● **Go to the Main Menu and give the** Work with... **command.**

The box labeled Desktop Index tells you what files are now in memory. You want to work with file Letter.

● **Select** Letter **and tap** (RETURN).

Now you are back at the Review/Add/Change screen for file Letter. Your joke is still on the invisible clipboard.

● **Place the cursor under the** S **at the beginning of the last sentence. Then type this sentence:**

Here's a knock-knock joke for you:

● **Tap** (RETURN) **at the end of the sentence.**

The cursor should still be under the S. This is where you want to insert your joke.

● **Give the Copy command again.**

● **This time, choose** From clipboard... **and tap** (RETURN).

There it is. The computer made a copy of the text block on the clipboard and put it into file Letter. The figure on the next page shows how your screen should look.

```
File: Letter                    REVIEW/ADD/CHANGE              Escape: Main Menu
=====|====|====|====|====|====|====|====|====|====|====|====|====|====|====|===

January 27, 1987

Dear Helen,

Hi.  This is the first letter I've ever written on a word
processing system.  I'm using the computer at my school and
a program called AppleWorks.

In a few weeks, we're also going to learn how to use the
computer to work with data bases and spreadsheets.  I don't
know what they are, but I guess they're pretty useful.

Here's a knock-knock joke for you:

    Knock, Knock!
          Who's there?
    Wendy
          Wendy who?
    Wendy wind blows, de cradle will rock...
-----------------------------------------------------------------------
Type entry or use ᶑ commands            Line 15  Column  1        -? for Help
```

Joke from file KnockKnock

The joke is still on the clipboard, so you can copy it into still other files if you want to.

● **Change the file name to** `MyLetter`. **Save it on your Data disk.**

Quick Check

5?   Suppose you want to copy a paragraph from one word processor file to another. After giving the Copy command, what option should you choose?

- -

6?   After using the Copy command to move a paragraph from one file to another, the paragraph is in three places. What are they?

- -

Other Uses of the Clipboard

Using the clipboard for editing makes many interesting things possible. You have just seen that the clipboard allows you to move a copy of a text block from one file to another file. You can also use the clipboard to insert many copies of a text block into the same file without selecting the original text block each time.

◆ **A simple example**   A new version of the previous example will show how to make many copies of the same text block. Suppose a word processor file contains the following text:

```
It was the best of times. worst of times. age of
wisdom. age of foolishness.
```

The goal is to edit the text so that it becomes

```
It was the best of times. It was the worst of times.
It was the age of wisdom. It was the age of foolishness.
```

To make these changes, you need to insert the same text block (It was the and the space after it) in three different places in the file. You *could* do this by using the Within document option of the Copy command. However, you would have to go through all the steps three times. There is an easier way.

◆ **Copy to clipboard**   The first step in making multiple copies is to put a copy of the selected text onto the clipboard. The figure below shows this process for the example just given.

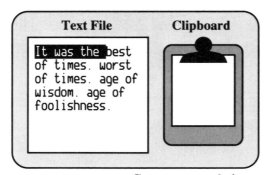
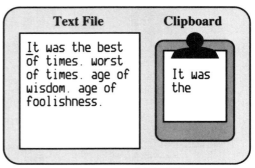

Copy command given,
To clipboard **chosen,**
text selected

(RETURN) **key tapped**

In the first frame the Copy command has been given and To clipboard has been chosen. The proper text block is selected. There is nothing on the clipboard now. In the second frame (RETURN) has been tapped. The copy is now on the clipboard. The text block in the file is no longer highlighted. That completes the process of putting material on the clipboard. The computer automatically returns to the Review/Add/Change screen, where you are free to do any of the things normally done there.

◆ **An important difference**   When you used the `Within document` option before, the computer automatically erased the clipboard after the block was copied. This is not true when you use the `To clipboard` option. Whatever you put on the clipboard remains there. The next step is to move text from the clipboard back into the file at new locations.

◆ **Copy from clipboard**   The next figure shows the steps needed to move a copy of text on the clipboard back into the file.

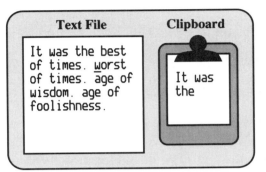 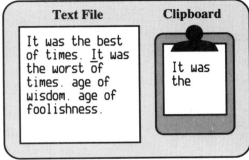

Cursor positioned,
Copy command given again   `From clipboard` **chosen**

    You begin by positioning the cursor at the first place where you want to insert a copy of the block now on the clipboard. The next step is to give the Copy command. The first frame shows these two steps. Notice that the clipboard still contains the text block you want inserted. The second frame shows what happens when you choose the `From clipboard` option. The computer inserts the contents of the clipboard at the cursor location in the file. However, the computer *does not* erase the clipboard.

◆ **More copies**   Now it should be clear why using the clipboard this way lets you make many copies of the same text block. Since the block remains on the clipboard, you can move the cursor to a new location in the file, give the Copy command, and choose `From clipboard`. The figure below shows this.

 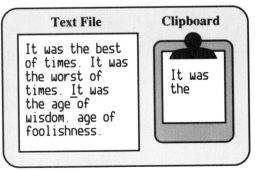

Cursor positioned,
Copy command given again   `From clipboard` **chosen again**

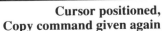

    Nothing has happened to the material on the clipboard. You can repeat these steps for as many copies as you choose.

◆ **Copying between files**   Once information is stored on the clipboard, it stays there even if you leave the Review/Add/Change screen. This makes it possible to copy information from one file to another. Here is how you did this:

1. Use the Copy command and `To clipboard` option to place on the clipboard the material to be moved.

2. Leave the Review/Add/Change screen and select another file.

3. Move the cursor where you want the copy to appear in the new file.

4. Give the Copy command and choose `From clipboard`.

That's all there is to it. The examples here have been very simple. In practice the clipboard allows you to move large quantities of information back and forth between AppleWorks files.

◆ **The Move command**   The `To clipboard` and `From clipboard` options can also be used with the Move command. The only difference is that the Move command erases the the text from its old location. With the `To clipboard` option, the computer erases the selected block from the file. With the `From clipboard` option, the computer erases the text from the clipboard.

◆ **Commands that change the clipboard**   You cannot see what is on the AppleWorks clipboard, so it is important to know what commands can change the information there. The Copy and Move commands are the main ones to watch out for. The `Within document` option always leaves the clipboard empty. The `To clipboard` option also erases the clipboard; then the computer puts new information there. The `From clipboard` option leaves the clipboard untouched when used with the Copy command; however when used with the Move command, the clipboard is erased. The table below sums up these rules.

Command	Option	Effect on Clipboard
Move or Copy	Within document	erased
Move or Copy	To clipboard	changed
Move	From clipboard	erased
Copy	From clipboard	unchanged

This brings you to the end of the regular activities. If you have time, do some of the On Your Own activities below. When you are finished, quit AppleWorks in the usual way. Throw away any changes you do not want to keep.

On Your Own

■ Load file MyJokes into memory. Add your own knock-knock jokes by first making several copies of the standard form and then editing each one.

■ Copy several more jokes from file MyJokes into file MyLetter. Send a copy of the expanded file MyLetter to the printer.

Review Questions

1. Suppose you want to make a copy of a block of five lines in a word processor file. What are the first two things you should do?

    ----

2. How do the Copy and Move commands differ in their effects?

    ----

3. In AppleWorks what is the clipboard?

    ----

4. You give the Copy command, choose `Within document`, select a block of text, and tap (RETURN). What happens?

    ----

5. After carrying out the steps in question 4, you move the cursor to a new location and tap (RETURN). What happens? What is on the clipboard afterward?

    ----

6. Suppose you give the Copy command, choose `To clipboard`, select a block of text, and tap (RETURN). What happens?

    ----

7. After carrying out the steps in question 6, you move the cursor to a new location, give the Copy command, and choose `From clipboard`. What happens? What is on the clipboard afterward?

    ----

8. A file contains a block of text that you want to copy and insert in many other places in the same file. What is the easiest way to do this?

    ----

9. How can you copy a block of text from one file into another file?

Goals

✔ Do prewriting and planning activities for a writing project.
✔ Use a word processor program to write a paper.
✔ Use word processor editing tools to revise a paper.

Choosing a Topic

◆
★

You have now learned all the important editing tools to use with Apple-Works word processor files. In this lab you will apply these tools while working on a writing project of your own.

◆ **Topics available**   You will have your choice of three topics to write about. The paragraphs below describe each of the topics. Read each paragraph and think about the ideas presented there.

1. **Using Word Processors for Writing**   In schools today most writing is done with pencil and paper. However, many students are learning to use computers and word processor programs. Some people believe that the computer should be used for most writing tasks in schools. Others are not so sure.

2. **Grade Requirements for Athletics and Band**   Some people say that students should have good grades in order to take part in athletics, band, and the like. A few states require students to have a grade of C or better in all courses before they can take part in extracurricular activities. Not everybody agrees with this.

3. **Different Driving Age for Males and Females**   Accident records in the United States show that young male drivers have many more ac-cidents than young females. Some people think that a fair solution to this problem would be to have a higher legal driving age for males than for females. Others disagree.

You probably have ideas of your own about one or more of these topics. You will soon have a chance to put those ideas into writing.

◆ **Writer's aids**   Getting started with a writing project is often difficult. On your Data disk there are three files, one for each of the topics above. These files will help you jot down a few ideas, answer some important questions, and plan your paper. This is a good approach whether you are using a computer or not. If you put your original thinking and planning into a word processor file, however, you can use editing tools to move a phrase or a group of sentences into the final paper without retyping. The first step in this lab is to load the proper file for the topic you have chosen.

Follow the Steps

● **Start the computer with AppleWorks.**

File Topic1 on your Data disk deals with using word processors in schools. File Topic2 is about grade requirements for athletics. Topic3 is about different legal driving ages for males and females.

● **Load the file for the topic you have chosen to write about.**

If you chose Topic1, for example, your screen would look like the figure below. The other files are similar.

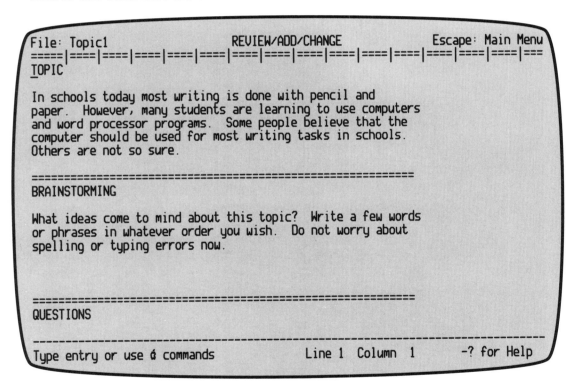

```
File: Topic1                 REVIEW/ADD/CHANGE              Escape: Main Menu
=====|====|====|====|====|====|====|====|====|====|====|====|====|====|===
TOPIC

In schools today most writing is done with pencil and
paper.  However, many students are learning to use computers
and word processor programs.  Some people believe that the
computer should be used for most writing tasks in schools.
Others are not so sure.


=================================================================
BRAINSTORMING

What ideas come to mind about this topic?  Write a few words
or phrases in whatever order you wish.  Do not worry about
spelling or typing errors now.




=================================================================
QUESTIONS

-------------------------------------------------------------------------
Type entry or use ⌂ commands            Line 1  Column  1      -? for Help
```

● **Use the Name command ⌘N to change the file name to** MyPaper.

At the top of the screen, you should see the same paragraph you read earlier when choosing this topic. Now is a good time to look at the rest of the file.

● **Scroll through the file and read the main headings.**

Each heading describes one step in the writing process.

Thinking about the Topic

As you see, the last step in the writing process is the actual writing. It is usually a mistake to start writing a paper without going through the earlier steps.

Follow the Steps

● **Scroll to the beginning of the file. Read the paragraph under** BRAINSTORMING.

Brainstorming means simply jotting down anything that comes to mind about the topic: words, phrases, ideas, and the like. This is always a good way to get started. It is not important at this point to worry about spelling, typing errors, or grammar. The purpose is to get ideas down where you can see them.

● **Move the cursor below the paragraph you just read.**

● **Type any words or phrases that come to mind. You can put each one on a different line or use dashes to separate them if you like.**

You should spend only two or three minutes on this task. You can always return later to add more ideas.

● **Scroll down so that you can read the section labeled** QUESTIONS.

In your brainstorming you probably thought of several arguments on both sides of the topic. The questions in this section should focus your attention on these arguments.

● **Read each question. In the space below the question, write a sentence or two that gives your answer.**

You should spend 10 or 15 minutes thinking about these questions and your answers. When you write your paper, you will probably be able to move many of the things you say now directly into the paper.

Planning the Paper

At this point you should have a good idea of the arguments on both sides of the topic you have chosen. Now it is time to think about the paper you will write.

Follow the Steps

● **Scroll to the** AUDIENCE **section of the file.**

Before beginning to write, it is important to decide on the audience. Are you trying to persuade another student, the school principal, a city official, or someone else?

```
┌──────────────────────────────────────────────────────────────────┐
│ File: MyPaper                  REVIEW/ADD/CHANGE        Escape: Main Menu │
│ =====|====|====|====|====|====|====|====|====|====|====|====|====|====|=== │
│ ════════════════════════════════════════════════════════════════════ │
│ AUDIENCE                                                           │
│                                                                    │
│ To whom are you writing?  Who should be convinced by what          │
│ you write?                                                         │
│                                                                    │
│                                                                    │
│ ════════════════════════════════════════════════════════════      │
│ IN A NUTSHELL                                                      │
│                                                                    │
│ Say in one or two sentences what you intend to do in this          │
│ paper.                                                             │
│                                                                    │
│                                                                    │
│ ════════════════════════════════════════════════════════════      │
│ PLANNING                                                          │
│                                                                    │
│ 1.  What is a good way to start your paper?                        │
│                                                                    │
│ _                                                                  │
│ ─────────────────────────────────────────────────────────────     │
│ Type entry or use ₵ commands          Line 66  Column  1    -? for Help │
└──────────────────────────────────────────────────────────────────┘
```

● **Write a few words to describe the readers that you will have in mind when you write your paper.**

Just as important as knowing to whom you are writing is having a clear and simple idea of what you intend to do.

● **Scroll to the next section in the file. Enter a few sentences to give a "nutshell" view of your purpose.**

Your nutshell description of the purpose of your paper will be helpful in both planning and writing. If you get bogged down in the details, a quick look back at your nutshell description will remind you what you were trying to do.

● **Scroll to the** PLANNING **section of the file.**

The last step before writing is to organize your thoughts. The questions in this section are a good starting point. You may decide to write an outline of your paper here or simply make a few notes to yourself about what will go in each part of the paper.

● **Enter your outline or notes in this section.**

You should spend five or ten minutes thinking about the organization of your paper and entering your outline or notes.

● **Use the Save command ⌘S to save a copy of file MyPaper on your Data disk.**

Writing the Paper

The hard work is over. You know your topic. You know your audience. You know the purpose of your paper. You have a plan for the organization of the paper. All that remains is to begin writing. (If you run out of time while writing your paper, be sure to save the final version of your file on your Data disk.)

Follow the Steps

● **Scroll to question 1 of the PLANNING section. Remind yourself how you intended to start the paper.**

● **Scroll to the end of the file. Begin writing.**

```
File: MyPaper              REVIEW/ADD/CHANGE           Escape: Main Menu
=====|====|====|====|====|====|====|====|====|====|====|====|====|====|===


  =======================================================
  PLANNING

  1.  What is a good way to start your paper?


  2.  What do you want to do in the body of your paper?


  3.  What final impressions do you want to leave with the
  reader of your paper?


  =======================================================
  WRITING

  Begin your paper here.
  _
  -----------------------------------------------------------------
Type entry or use ⌂ commands              Line 78  Column  1      -? for Help
```

Your goal should be to get your thoughts expressed as complete sentences. Don't be concerned with spelling errors now. Don't spend time making small corrections.

- ● **When you have finished the opening of your paper, scroll back to the** PLANNING **section and decide whether you have done what you intended to do.**

- ● **Repeat this process for the body and final part of your paper.**

When writing the body of your paper, you will probably want to go back to the QUESTIONS section and look at the arguments on both sides of your topic. If you find good sentences in your answers, you can use the block-editing tools to move the sentences into your paper.

- ● **Use the Save command to move a copy of file MyPaper to your Data disk.**

Revising and Editing

At this point you have a first draft of your paper. It should contain all the ideas and arguments that you wanted to include. Now is the time to become a critic.

Follow the Steps

- ● **With file MyPaper on the Review/Add/Change screen, scroll back to the** IN A NUTSHELL **section. Review what you intended to do in your paper.**

- ● **Read your paper and see whether it does what you wanted it to do.**

- ● **Scroll to the** PLANNING **section. Review the organization you planned. Compare this with what you wrote.**

- ● **Use the AppleWorks editing tools to revise and improve your paper.**

- ● **Reread your paper and make any further revisions.**

Your paper should be looking better. Now it is time to focus on details.

- ● **Read the paper carefully from the beginning. Look for spelling errors and grammatical mistakes. Make any corrections needed.**

The last step is to make a printed copy of your paper. Before doing that, you will want to think about the appearance of the paper: the size of the margins, line spacing, a title, and the like. Chapter 3 deals with these topics. At the end of Chapter 3, you will make a printed copy of file MyPaper. Until then you are free to do more work on your paper.

- ● **Save a copy of file MyPaper on your Data disk. Then quit AppleWorks.**

Important   Be sure to save this file and keep it on your Data disk. In Chapter 3 you will come back to this file, make additional changes, and print the final version.

The Writing Task

In this chapter you have learned to use the AppleWorks word processor program as an aid to writing and editing. Other word processor programs have different commands, but they all do the same basic things. These programs are making fundamental changes in the way people do writing tasks.

◆ **Writing skills** Probably the most important skill we ever learn is the skill of using language—especially written language. As the number of farm and factory jobs continues to shrink, more and more people seek work in places where they must read and write well: business offices, government offices, schools, laboratories, and the like. That is why schools devote so much time to reading and writing activities.

◆ **Writing problems** A few lucky people find that writing comes easily to them. Most of the rest of us think of writing as hard work. Even when we know what we think or feel about a topic, we have a lot of trouble getting those thoughts and feelings down on paper. We often get off on the wrong foot, forget where we are going, forget the audience we are writing for, get bogged down in unimportant details, and lose our way. Often we are also worried about spelling and appearance when we should be thinking about what we want to say.

◆ **Prewriting** People who write well and do a lot of writing face these very same problems every day, but they have learned ways to solve them. One successful approach is to spend more time in "prewriting activities:" the brainstorming, nutshelling, and planning steps that you used in the previous lab. Here the focus is on getting the ideas down on paper, thinking about goals, and developing a basic plan of attack—without worrying about grammar, spelling, and punctuation.

◆ **Writing** The time spent on prewriting activities is paid back with interest when the writing begins. Notes and plans scribbled on paper can be referred to while writing. The chances of getting lost or bogged down in details or forgetting the audience are far less now. The writer can pay attention to the job of putting ideas into complete sentences and building paragraphs.

◆ **Revising** Successful writers know that their first draft will have to be rewritten a few times before the job is done. After the first draft it is time to look for spelling and grammar errors, missing punctuation, sentences that are too long or too short, better ways to say the same thing, possible changes in the order of paragraphs, and so on. These revsions are what make the difference between a poor writing job and one that looks polished and professional.

◆ **Before the computer**   With only pencil and paper or typewriter, the writing process is slow and painful. Ideas written down during the prewriting stage have to be rewritten during the writing stage. Each new revision means copying large sections of the previous draft that did not need changes—or else using scissors and tape to move the old sections into the new draft.

◆ **After the computer**   Word processor software has not changed the writing process in any basic way; but it has removed a lot of the pain. As you saw in the lab, you can do all your prewriting activities at the computer. If you get a good sentence or two down while brainstorming, there is no penalty: Later you can use block-editing commands to move the sentence into your paper. Revising is so easy with a word processor program that there is no excuse for leaving flaws in a paper. You can make changes whenever you like and then print a fresh copy.

Review
Questions

1. Why are good writing skills more important today than they were in the past?

   ----

2. What are some examples of things that make writing a difficult task?

   ----

3. What goes on in the prewriting stage of creating a paper?

   ----

4. Why do prewriting activities save time when the actual writing begins?

   ----

5. Why is it important to make revisions after the first draft of a paper?

   ----

6. How can the computer make prewriting activities easier to use when the actual writing begins?

   ----

7. How can the computer aid in the process of revising a paper?

Keyboard Commands

⌐C, **Copy**	Make a copy of a block of text and insert it in a new place in a word processor file.
⌐D, **Delete**	Delete a text block from a word processor file.
⌐E, **Edit mode**	Switch between exchange mode and insert mode.
⌐F, **Find**	Find a word, phrase, or other series of characters in a word processor file. The search begins at the cursor position.
⌐M, **Move**	Delete a block of text and insert it in a new place in a word processor file.
⌐N, **Name**	Change the name of the file now visible on the Review/Add/Change screen.
⌐P, **Print**	Print a word processor file.
⌐R, **Replace**	Find a word, phrase, or other series of characters in a word processor file and replace it with another series of characters. The search begins at the cursor position.
⌐S, **Save**	Save on a disk a copy of the file now visible on the Review/Add/Change screen.
⌐Y, **Yank**	Erase all characters from the cursor to the end of a text line.
⌐1 **through** ⌐9	Move the cursor to the beginning or the end of a file, or to points between.
⌐↓, ⌐↑	Move the cursor down or up one full screen at a time.
⌐←, ⌐→	Move the cursor left or right one word at a time.
(RETURN)	End a paragraph or enter a blank line into a word processor file.

New Ideas

blob	A shape displayed on the computer screen at the place in an AppleWorks word processor file where (RETURN) was tapped.
case sensitive text	A mode used when searching for words or phrases. Uppercase and lowercase letters are treated as different letters.
clipboard	A part of memory used to hold information temporarily. Blocks of text can be moved to and from the clipboard when editing.
delete	Remove information from a file.
edit	Add information to a file or delete information from it.

edit mode   In AppleWorks the way in which typed characters are added to a file. See *exchange mode* and *insert mode*.

exchange mode   An edit mode. Typed characters take the place of those at the cursor position.

hard copy   A copy on paper of all or part of the information in a computer file.

insert   Put information into a file at any location. No information is removed from the file.

insert mode   An edit mode. Typed characters are inserted at the position of the cursor.

search   Find a pattern of text in a word processor file.

search and replace   Find one pattern of text in a word processor file and substitute another pattern for it.

text block   Any group of consecutive characters in a word processor file. A block may contain as little as a single character. A block may extend over many text lines.

wordwrap   Automatic moving of a word to the next line when it is too long to fit on the current line.

Formatting the Output

In Chapter 2 you learned to use all the tools needed to create, edit, and revise word processor files. When the writing process is over, it is time to think about the appearance of your words on the printed page. This chapter introduces new tools for controlling the way word processor files will appear when printed.

◆ **Appearance** Take a moment to look carefully at a few pages of this book. The paper has a certain size. Notice the margins. Notice the spacing between lines. Some text is indented differently from the rest. Other text is centered between the margins. Some words are printed in boldface type or other special typefaces. Page numbers appear at the tops of most pages along with other information that is repeated for many pages.

◆ **Content** The same information could have been printed on paper of a different size, with different margins and spacing between lines, in a different typeface, and so on. In other words the appearance of printed text and its information content are two different things. During the writing and editing of a paper, you should be thinking mainly about content. When the content is complete, you should start planning how the paper will appear when printed.

◆ **AppleWorks tools** The lab work in this chapter introduces the AppleWorks tools for controlling page layout: the size of the paper and the width of each of the four margins. You will also learn commands for controlling the space between lines, centering text between margins, printing phrases in boldface, and underlining phrases. Later you will find out how to print page numbers and other information on each page.

◆ **Application** Once all these new tools are mastered, you will put them to use. You will add the new formatting commands to the writing project you created and edited in Chapter 2. Then you will send the formatted file to the printer and see the results.

Goals

✔ Find out where page breaks will occur when a word processor file is printed.

✔ Use printer options to specify the paper size.

Calculating Page Breaks

You have learned all the tools needed to enter text into a word processor file and edit it. This chapter introduces the tools needed for controlling the appearance of a file when it is printed. These tools are called **format commands**.

● **Start the computer with AppleWorks.**

● **Load file Dickens from your Data disk.**

● **Give the ⌒9 command to go to the end of the file.**

This is a fairly long file. The cursor is on line 114. You might wonder how many pages would be needed to print the file. Here's how to find out.

● **Give the Calculate command ⌒K.**

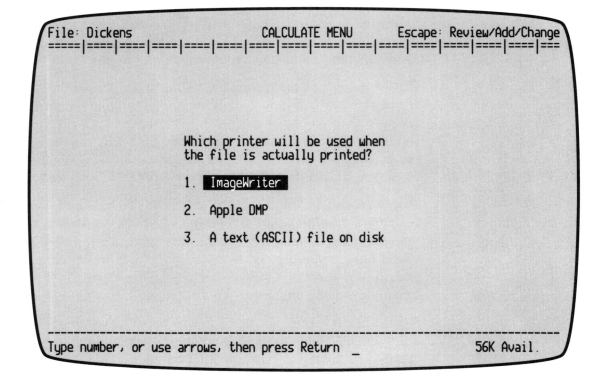

```
File: Dickens              CALCULATE MENU       Escape: Review/Add/Change
=====|====|====|====|====|====|====|====|====|====|====|====|====|====|===




              Which printer will be used when
              the file is actually printed?

              1.  ImageWriter

              2.  Apple DMP

              3.  A text (ASCII) file on disk



-----------------------------------------------------------------------
Type number, or use arrows, then press Return  _            56K Avail.
```

The computer asks you which printer will be used when the file is printed. For this lab pretend that you are using an ImageWriter printer. (You are not going to print the file now. For printing you would choose the printer actually connected to your computer.)

● **Select** ImageWriter **and tap** (RETURN).

The computer calculates the length of each page and shows the page divisions. (These page markers are temporary; they go away as soon as you begin editing the file.) As you can see, file Dickens will fill two pages and put five lines on the third page.

● **Move the cursor to last line of page 1.**

As you see, the cursor is on line 54. In other words the computer puts 54 lines on a page. Later you will see how to change the number of lines on a page.

```
File: Dickens              REVIEW/ADD/CHANGE          Escape: Main Menu
=====|====|====|====|====|====|====|====|====|====|====|====|====|====|====|===
received through any of the chickens of the Cock-lane brood.

France, less favoured on the whole as to matters spiritual
than her sister of the shield and trident, rolled with
exceeding smoothness down hill, making paper money and
spending it.  Under the guidance of her Christian pastors,
she entertained herself, besides, with such humane
achievements as sentencing a youth to have his hands cut
off, his tongue torn out with pincers, and his body burned
alive, because he had not kneeled down in the rain to do
honour to a dirty procession of monks which passed within
his view, at a distance of some fifty or sixty yards.  It is
likely enough that, rooted in the woods of France and
- - - - - - - - - - - - - - - End of Page 1 - - - - - - - - - - - - - - -
Norway, there were growing trees, when that sufferer was put
to death, already marked by the Woodman, Fate, to come down
and be sawn into boards, to make a certain movable framework
with a sack and a knife in it, terrible in history.  It is
likely enouygh that in the rough outhouses of some tillers of
the heavy lands adjacent to Paris, there were sheltered from
--------------------------------------------------------------------------
Type entry or use ⚡ commands        Line 54  Column  1        -? for Help
```

Page marker

There is a quick way to move from page to page after you calculate the page breaks.

● **Give the Find command** (⚡F)**. Read the list of options at the bottom of the screen.**

This is the same Find screen that you used earlier when searching for text. You can also search for the ends of pages.

● **Select the** Page **option and tap** (RETURN).

The new prompt asks you to enter a page number. Find the end of page 2.

104

● **Type** 2 **and tap** (RETURN).

There it is. The End of Page 2 marker is at the middle of the screen. (Also, notice that the computer now displays the (RETURN) blobs.)

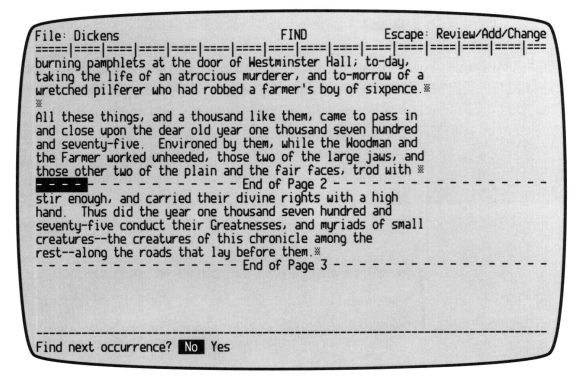

```
File: Dickens                    FIND         Escape: Review/Add/Change
=====|====|====|====|====|====|====|====|====|====|====|====|====|====|===
burning pamphlets at the door of Westminster Hall; to-day,
taking the life of an atrocious murderer, and to-morrow of a
wretched pilferer who had robbed a farmer's boy of sixpence.※
※
All these things, and a thousand like them, came to pass in
and close upon the dear old year one thousand seven hundred
and seventy-five.  Environed by them, while the Woodman and
the Farmer worked unheeded, those two of the large jaws, and
those other two of the plain and the fair faces, trod with ※
- - - - - - - - - - - - - - - End of Page 2 - - - - - - - - - - - - - - -
stir enough, and carried their divine rights with a high
hand.  Thus did the year one thousand seven hundred and
seventy-five conduct their Greatnesses, and myriads of small
creatures--the creatures of this chronicle among the
rest--along the roads that lay before them.※
- - - - - - - - - - - - - - - End of Page 3 - - - - - - - - - - - - - - -

------------------------------------------------------------------------
Find next occurrence?  No  Yes
```

The prompt at the bottom of the screen is misleading. There is no next occurrence of page 2. If you chose Yes, the computer would simply tell you that there is not another page 2.

● **Tap** (RETURN) **to choose** No.

Now the cursor is at the end of page 2. You have searched forward through the file to find the end of page 2. Can you search backward? Try it.

● **Give the Find command again. Choose** Page **and tap** (RETURN).

● **At the** Page number? **prompt, type 1 and tap** (RETURN). **Then tap** (RETURN) **again to end the search.**

The cursor is at the end of page 1. As you can see, it does not matter where the cursor is when you search for a page break. The situation is different when you search for text. The search for text always begins at the cursor position and moves forward in the file.

● **Use the Find command to locate the end of page 3. Tap** (RETURN) **to end the search.**

Notice that the Find Page command has left the file with the (RETURN) blobs showing. AppleWorks has a command to make the blobs either visible or invisible.

● **Give the Zoom command** (⌨Z).

Now the blobs are gone.

● **Give the Zoom command again.**

Now the blobs are back. Sometimes when editing it is important to know where (RETURN) was tapped. You can use the Zoom command to make the (RETURN) blobs visible.

Quick Check

1?   Suppose you want to see where each page will end in a word processor file in memory. What steps should you take?

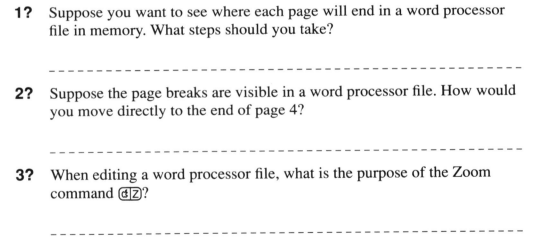

2?   Suppose the page breaks are visible in a word processor file. How would you move directly to the end of page 4?

3?   When editing a word processor file, what is the purpose of the Zoom command (⌨Z)?

Laying Out the Page

◆
★

When planning the appearance of a printed page, the first things to think about are the format commands that tell the computer what size paper will be used and how big the margins should be. These numbers define the **page layout** of the document.

◆ **Paper size**   The figure below shows the general layout of any printed page. The size of the paper is given by two numbers: the paper width and the paper length. In the United States most paper is 8½ inches wide and 11 inches long. Most computer printers handle this size and other sizes as well. Whatever size you use when printing a word processor document, you must tell the computer the width and length of your paper.

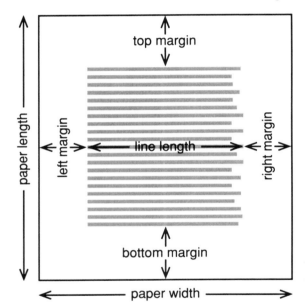

Main distances that affect the layout of the printed page.

◆ **Margins**   The white spaces that border the text on a printed page are called **margins**. The margins are given by four numbers: the top, bottom, left, and right amounts. These amounts tell the distances from the four edges of the paper to the block of text printed on the page.

◆ **Line length**   Each printed line begins just to the right of the left margin and stops before reaching the right margin. It is easy to calculate the maximum **line length**. You simply subtract the sum of the left and right margins from the paper width. For example, suppose the paper width is 8½ inches, the left margin is 1 inch, and the right margin is also 1 inch. Then the line length would be 6½ inches.

Specifying the Paper Size

In its present form, file Dickens fills two 54-line pages plus a few lines on the third page. How did AppleWorks decide where the page breaks should occur? To answer this question you must first explore the Printer Option screen. This screen contains a list of all the commands that affect the format of a file when it is printed. In AppleWorks, format commands are called **printer options**.

Follow the Steps

● **Move the cursor to the beginning of the file. If the RETURN blobs are hidden, give the Zoom command.**

● **Give the Options command ⌕O.**

You are now at the Printer Options screen. The prompt area on this screen takes up 11 lines, beginning with the highlighted line.

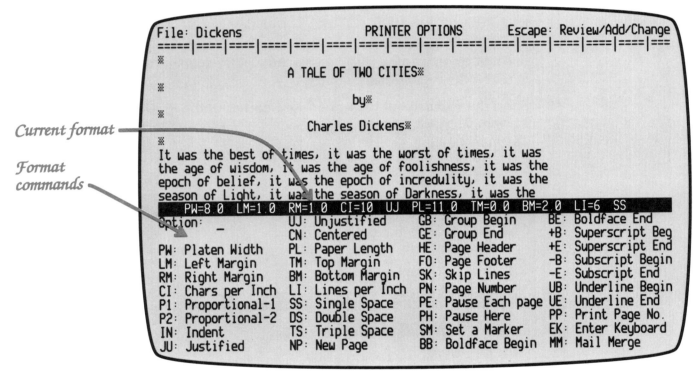

Current format

Format commands

The computer is waiting for you to enter a printer option. As you can see there are dozens of options. (Older versions of AppleWorks do not have the Mail Merge option.) You will learn about many of these options in this chapter. For now focus on just two of them: Platen Width and Paper Length.

● **In the list of options, find the abbreviations for** Platen Width **and** Paper Length.

● **Find these same abbreviations in the highlighted line.**

The numbers in the highlighted line show that the platen width is now 8 inches, and the paper length is 11 inches. (*Platen width* here means the same thing as *paper width*.) In other words the computer expects your printer to use paper that is 8 inches wide and 11 inches long. In fact most printers use paper that is 8½ inches by 11 inches. Use a printer option to tell the computer to change the platen width to 8½ inches (for the computer you will use the decimal form 8.5).

● **Type** PW **and tap** (RETURN).

You choose an option by typing its two-letter abbreviation. You can use either capital or lowercase letters. The computer is waiting for you to enter the new value for the paper width.

● **Type** 8.5 **and tap** (RETURN). **Look at the top line of the file.**

You have now inserted a printer option at the beginning of file Dickens. The row of hyphens shows where the option is inserted. The message after the hyphens tells what option is there. This option tells the computer to set the platen width to 8½ inches. Also notice the new value for PW in the highlighted line in the prompt area. There are no more printer options to add now, so return to the Review/Add/Change screen.

● **Read the message at the upper right corner of the Printer Options screen. Do what it says.**

The printer option and the (RETURN) blobs are now visible in the file.

● **Give the Zoom command.**

Now they are hidden.

● **Give the Zoom command again.**

Now they are visible once more. See how many pages are now needed to print the file.

● **Give the Calculate command** (⌘K), **choose** ImageWriter, **and tap** (RETURN).

● **Move the cursor to the end of the file.**

The file will now fit on two pages when it is printed. This should not surprise you. With wider paper, each line can be ½ inch longer, so fewer lines are needed.

The Platen Width and Paper Length printer options allow you to print on any size paper you want. For example, suppose you wanted to print file Dickens on paper that was only 7 inches long. Here is what to do:

● **Move the cursor to the beginning of the file.**

● **Give the Options command** (⌘O). **Type** PL **and tap** (RETURN). **Type** 7 **and tap** (RETURN).

This inserts a `Paper Length` printer option at the beginning of the file. In the highlighted line, notice the new value for `PL`.

● **Return to the Review/Add/Change screen. Give the Calculate command. Go to the end of the file.**

Since the paper is shorter, it will take more pages to print file Dickens. Next see how to change the `Paper Length` option back to 11 inches. You might think that the easiest way is to edit the `Paper Length` printer option at the top of the screen.

● **Go to the beginning of the file. Try to use the editing tools you have learned to change** `7.0` **to** `11.0`.

No luck. You cannot edit a printer option in a file. You must first delete the option and, if necessary, use the Option command to insert a new one.

● **With the cursor at the** `Paper Length` **option line, give the Delete command** Ⓓ Ⓓ **.**

The computer highlights the entire printer option line.

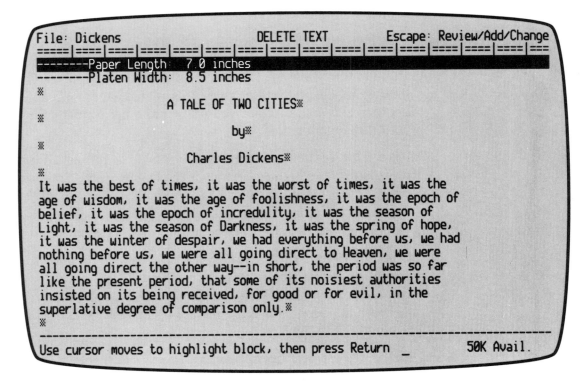

```
File: Dickens                   DELETE TEXT         Escape: Review/Add/Change
=====|====|====|====|====|====|====|====|====|====|====|====|====|====|====|===
--------Paper Length:  7.0 inches
--------Platen Width:  8.5 inches
  ※
                      A TALE OF TWO CITIES※
  ※
                             by※
  ※
                        Charles Dickens※
  ※
It was the best of times, it was the worst of times, it was the
age of wisdom, it was the age of foolishness, it was the epoch of
belief, it was the epoch of incredulity, it was the season of
Light, it was the season of Darkness, it was the spring of hope,
it was the winter of despair, we had everything before us, we had
nothing before us, we were all going direct to Heaven, we were
all going direct the other way--in short, the period was so far
like the present period, that some of its noisiest authorities
insisted on its being received, for good or for evil, in the
superlative degree of comparison only.※
  ※
----------------------------------------------------------------------
Use cursor moves to highlight block, then press Return _         50K Avail.
```

Since the highlighted line is the text block you want to delete, you needn't use the arrow keys to highlight any other text.

● **Tap** RETURN **to complete the deletion.**

Now the printer option line is gone. With no `Paper Length` option in the file, the computer assumes that you will be using paper 11 inches long.

Quick Check

4?   Suppose you want to enter a printer option at the beginning of a file. What steps should you take?

_____

5?   How do you remove a printer option from a file?

_____

6?   Suppose you have set the platen width to 5 inches. What does that tell the computer?

_____

More About AppleWorks Format Commands

Now is a good time to review what you have learned about format commands. To tell the computer how you want the printed page to appear, you must insert these commands directly into your word processor file. In AppleWorks format commands are known as printer options.

◆   **Placing the format command**   Before using any format command, you must decide where you want it to appear in your file. Many format commands apply to the whole file. They should be used only once and should be placed at the beginning of the file. Examples include the `Platen Width` and `Paper Length` commands. Later you will learn other format commands that are often used throughout a file.

◆   **Inserting format commands**   To add a format command to your word processor file, you must first place the cursor where you want the command inserted. After giving the Options command, you insert the command by typing its two-letter abbreviation and tapping (RETURN). Some format commands, such as `Platen Width` and `Paper Length`, also require you to enter a number.

◆   **Seeing format commands**   Once a format command is given, it becomes part of your file. AppleWorks allows you to see all the format commands in a word processor file. When you first load a word processor file into memory, any format commands in the file are invisible. If you then give the Zoom command, the (RETURN) blobs and format commands all appear.

◆   **Deleting format commands**   In your lab work you saw that you cannot use (DELETE) to edit a printer option that is already in a file. To change a printer option, you must first remove it entirely. You do this by putting the cursor anywhere in the line containing the printer option, giving the Delete command (⌐D), and tapping (RETURN). Then you insert the new printer option into the file.

This completes the regular activities in this lab. If you have time, do some of the On Your Own activities on the next page. Then quit AppleWorks as usual. Throw away the changes to file Dickens.

On Your Own

■ Load file BusinessLetter from your Data disk. This is the form of a standard business letter. Change it into your personal form so that it contains your actual name and address. Change the file name to MyLetterForm. Save it.

■ With file MyLetterForm on the Review/Add/Change screen, give the Zoom command. Look at each of the format commands. See whether you can understand what each one tells the computer.

Review Questions

1. What is the difference between editing and formatting a word processor file?

- -

2. Why does the computer need to know the length of the paper a word processor file is to be printed on?

- -

3. In AppleWorks what paper width is assumed if you do not tell the computer otherwise?

- -

4. What three numbers determine the length of a printed line?

- -

5. How do you insert a printer option at a particular place in a file?

- -

6. Suppose you have just loaded an AppleWorks word processor file into memory. How can you see what printer options are in the file?

- -

7. Suppose a word processor file contains the printer option `Paper Length: 8.0 inches`. You want to change the page length to 11 inches. How would you do this?

- -

8. Why does the computer automatically remove any page break markers when you insert new text into a word processor file?

- -

Goals

✔ Use printer options to set the margins.
✔ Use printer options to center text.
✔ Print a file that contains printer options.

Setting the Margins

◆
★

In the previous lab you learned how to insert format commands into a word processor file. Using the `Platen Width` and `Paper Length` printer options, you told the computer what paper size the file was to be printed on. In the present lab you will explore several more AppleWorks format commands.

Follow the Steps

● **Start the computer with AppleWorks.**

● **Load file Dickens from your Data disk.**

You will soon be making changes in this file. Now is a good time to change the name of the file so you can save your work.

● **Give the Name command ⓒN. Use the Yank command ⓒY to erase the old name. Type** `Tale` **and tap** ⦅RETURN⦆.

As a review you will insert a `Platen Width` command at the beginning of file Tale. Recall that you insert format commands by first moving the cursor to the place the command is to be inserted. Then you give the Options command ⓒO and enter the proper format command.

● **With the cursor at the beginning of file Tale, set the platen width to 8.5 inches.**

● **Go back to the Review/Add/Change screen. Give the Zoom command.**

The top part of file Tale should look like this:

Format command ——

```
File: Tale                  REVIEW/ADD/CHANGE          Escape: Main Menu
=====|====|====|====|====|====|====|====|====|====|====|====|====|====|====|===
--------Platen Width: 8.5 inches
▓
              A TALE OF TWO CITIES▓
▓
                    by▓
▓
             Charles Dickens▓
▓
```

Now for something new. When you write or type a paper, you don't fill the whole sheet; you leave margins on all four edges. AppleWorks has printer options that let you decide how wide you want the margins to be. Usually you want to have the same margins apply to the whole file. Therefore the margin format commands belong at the beginning of the file.

● **Move the cursor just below the printer option at the beginning of the file. Give the Options command ⒹⓄ.**

● **In the highlighted line, check the values for platen width and paper length.**

The platen width should be 8.5 inches and the paper length should be 11 inches. (If not, change them to these values now.)

● **Find the abbreviations for the four** ...Margin **printer options. In the highlighted line, check the values for these four options.**

At present, the left and right margins are 1 inch each. The top margin is 0. The bottom margin is 2 inches. A top margin of 0 means that printing will begin at the very top of the page. Normally this is not what you want. Make the top margin 1 inch.

● **Type** TM **and tap** ⟨RETURN⟩. **Type** 1 **and tap** ⟨RETURN⟩. **Go back to the Review/Add/Change screen.**

```
File: Tale                    REVIEW/ADD/CHANGE          Escape: Main Menu
====|====|====|====|====|====|====|====|====|====|====|====|====|====|===
--------Platen Width:  8.5 inches
--------Top Margin:  1.0 inches
▨
                         A TALE OF TWO CITIES▨
▨
                                  by▨
▨
                            Charles Dickens▨
```

You have inserted a Top Margin printer option just below the Platen Width option. See what this new margin does to the number of pages needed to print the file.

● **Give the Calculate command ⒹⓀ. Go to the end of the file.**

Before you changed the top margin, the file could be printed on two pages. The new top margin means that fewer lines can be printed on each page, so it takes three pages to print the file now. However, there is an easy way to fit the file onto two pages again. The bottom margin is now 2 inches. Reducing it to 1 inch will allow more lines to be printed on each page.

● **Insert a** Bottom Margin **printer option just below the** Top Margin **option. Make the width of the margin 1 inch.**

● **Find how many pages will be needed to print the file now.**

Once again the file can be printed on two pages. Next make changes to the left and right margins.

● **Go to the beginning of the file. Make certain that you have inserted the three printer options shown in the figure.**

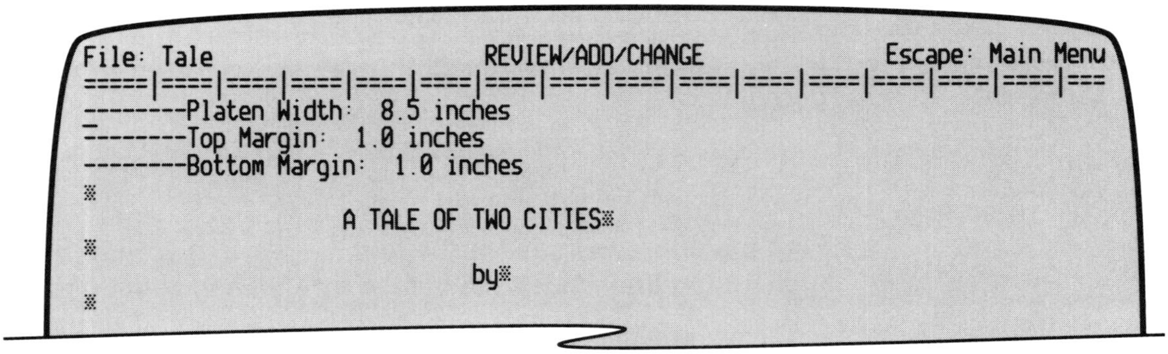

```
File: Tale                    REVIEW/ADD/CHANGE            Escape: Main Menu
=====|====|====|====|====|====|====|====|====|====|====|====|====|====|===
--------Platen Width:  8.5 inches
--------Top Margin:  1.0 inches
--------Bottom Margin:  1.0 inches
▓
              A TALE OF TWO CITIES▓
▓
                     by▓
▓
```

● **Move the cursor to the end of the first line in the first paragraph.**

The information at the bottom of the screen shows that the last character is in column 63. See what happens if you make the right margin wider.

● **Move the cursor just below the three printer options at the beginning of the file. Insert a** Right Margin **printer option. Make the margin 2 inches.**

● **At the Review/Add/Change screen, move the cursor to the end of the first line of the first paragraph.**

The last character in the first line is now at column 55.

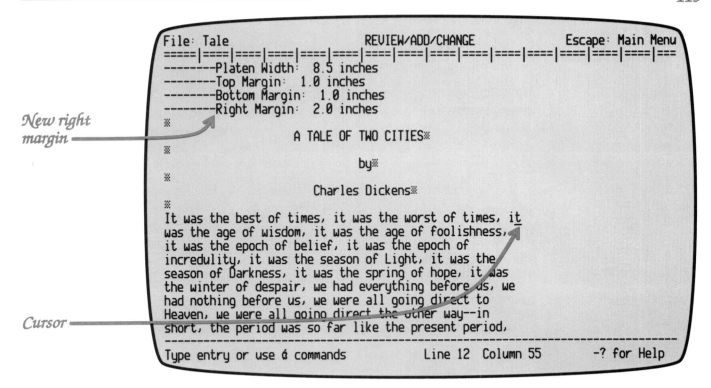

New right margin

Cursor

As you see, when you increase the right margin, the lines become shorter. Now change the left margin.

● **Put the cursor just below the printer options. Insert a** `Left Margin` **printer option with a value of 2 inches.**

● **Tap** (ESC) **to return to the Review/Add/Change screen.**

● **If necessary scroll to the beginning of the file.**

Your screen should look like the figure on the next page.

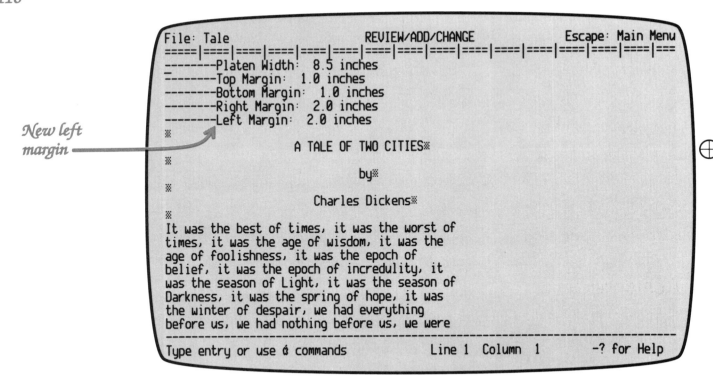

New left margin —

```
File: Tale                    REVIEW/ADD/CHANGE           Escape: Main Menu
=====|====|====|====|====|====|====|====|====|====|====|====|====|====|====|===
---------Platen Width:  8.5 inches
---------Top Margin:  1.0 inches
---------Bottom Margin:  1.0 inches
---------Right Margin:  2.0 inches
---------Left Margin:  2.0 inches
  ※
                       A TALE OF TWO CITIES※
  ※
                            by※
  ※
                       Charles Dickens※
  ※
It was the best of times, it was the worst of
times, it was the age of wisdom, it was the
age of foolishness, it was the epoch of
belief, it was the epoch of incredulity, it
was the season of Light, it was the season of
Darkness, it was the spring of hope, it was
the winter of despair, we had everything
before us, we had nothing before us, we were
-------------------------------------------------------------------------
Type entry or use ᗌ commands          Line 1  Column  1         -? for Help
```

Once again the lines have shortened. The left margin itself does not appear on the screen, but if you printed this file now, the lines would begin 2 inches from the left edge of the paper and would stop 2 inches from the right edge. See how many pages it will take to print the file with these short lines.

● **Use the Calculate command to see how many pages will be needed.**

With these printer options it will take three pages to print the file.

◆ **Effect of commands on output**   Notice that format commands tell the computer how a word processor file should look when it is printed. In other words these commands mainly affect the output of the word processor program, not the screen appearance of the file. For example, the Top Margin and Bottom Margin commands do *not* cause margins to appear on the screen, but they *do* create proper margins when the file is printed.

◆ **WYSIWYG**   Some word processor programs are known as "what-you-see-is-what-you-get" (or **WYSIWYG**) programs. They attempt to show on the screen exactly what the printed document will look like. Other word processor programs make no such attempt. The AppleWorks word processor program might be called WYSIMOLWYG: What you see is *more or less* what you get. For example, line lengths shown on the screen are the same as those on the printed page; however, margins appear only on the printed page, not on the screen.

Quick Check

1? If you do not insert printer options into a file, how wide will the top and bottom margins be when the file is printed?

2? If you do not insert printer options into a file, how wide will the left and right margins be when the file is printed?

3? Suppose you have set the left margin to 2 inches. What does that mean when you print the file?

Centering Text

When writing a paper you often want to center some of the text on the page. For example, you may want the title of the paper to be centered over the rest of the text. AppleWorks has a printer option for doing this.

Follow the Steps

● **Move the cursor to the beginning of file Dickens.**

Your screen should look like the previous figure. Notice that the three lines of heading are no longer centered over the rest of the text. This is so because the lines were originally centered by typing spaces before each heading. With the new margins these spaces put the headings in the wrong place. There is a better way to center text. First remove the spaces at the beginning of each of the three heading lines.

● **Move the cursor to the left end of the line containing** A TALE OF TWO CITIES.

● **Give the Delete command ⌐D. Highlight all the spaces at the beginning of the line.**

Your screen should look like the figure on the next page.

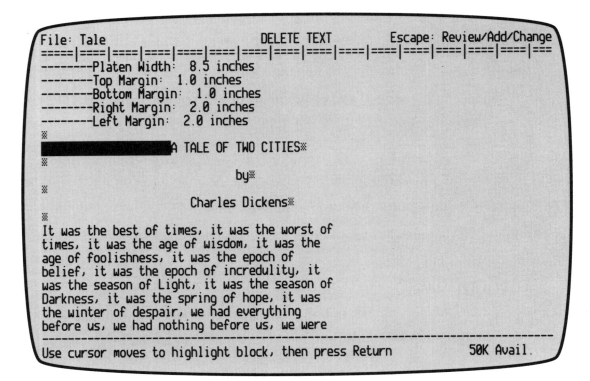

File: Tale   DELETE TEXT   Escape: Review/Add/Change
=====|====|====|====|====|====|====|====|====|====|====|====|====|====|====|===
---------Platen Width: 8.5 inches
---------Top Margin: 1.0 inches
---------Bottom Margin: 1.0 inches
---------Right Margin: 2.0 inches
---------Left Margin: 2.0 inches
※
███████████████████████A TALE OF TWO CITIES※
※
                        by※
※
                  Charles Dickens※
※
It was the best of times, it was the worst of
times, it was the age of wisdom, it was the
age of foolishness, it was the epoch of
belief, it was the epoch of incredulity, it
was the season of Light, it was the season of
Darkness, it was the spring of hope, it was
the winter of despair, we had everything
before us, we had nothing before us, we were

Use cursor moves to highlight block, then press Return   50K Avail.

- **Tap (RETURN) to delete the spaces.**

    Now A TALE OF TWO CITIES should begin at the left edge of the screen. The leading spaces are gone.

- **Use the same method to delete the leading spaces in the other two heading lines.**

    Now each line of the heading starts at the left edge of the screen. The next step is to insert a printer option to center these lines.

- **Move the cursor to the beginning of the first heading line.**

- **Give the Option command. Find the abbreviation for the Centered printer option.**

- **Type CN and tap (RETURN).**

    Things look pretty good. Now there is a Centered printer option line just above the first heading line. The three lines in the heading are now centered properly between the margins.

- **Tap (ESC) to return to the Review/Add/Change screen.**

    There seems to be a problem.

```
File: Tale                  REVIEW/ADD/CHANGE               Escape: Main Menu
=====|====|====|====|====|====|====|====|====|====|====|====|====|===
--------Top Margin:  1.0 inches
--------Bottom Margin:  1.0 inches
--------Right Margin:  2.0 inches
--------Left Margin:  2.0 inches
▓
--------Centered
-
            A TALE OF TWO CITIES▓
▓
                  by▓
▓
            Charles Dickens▓
▓
It was the best of times, it was the worst of
times, it was the age of wisdom, it was the
  age of foolishness, it was the epoch of
belief, it was the epoch of incredulity, it
was the season of Light, it was the season of
Darkness, it was the spring of hope, it was
   the winter of despair, we had everything
before us, we had nothing before us, we were
--------------------------------------------------------------------
Type entry or use ⌶ commands          Line 7  Column  1        -? for Help
```

All lines centered

- **Scroll to the the end of the file and back.**

    Now *all* the lines in the file are centered between the two margins. You wanted to center only the three heading lines. You need a way to turn off the centering after the headings.

- **Place the cursor just below the third line of the headings.**

- **Give the Option command.**

    The printer option just before Centered is the one you need. It tells the computer to start each line at the left margin.

- **Type UJ and tap (RETURN). Tap (ESC) to return to the Review/Add/Change screen.**

    Now the rest of the lines in the file are no longer centered. You can center any group of lines in a file by bracketing the lines with the Centered and Un-justified printer options as you did here. Next see what happens to your centered headings when you change the margins.

- **Scroll to the beginning of the file. Use the Delete command to remove the Right Margin... printer option.**

    Now the lines are longer, but the headings remain centered.

- **Use the Delete command to remove the Left Margin... printer option.**

    Again the lines are longer, and again the headings remain centered over the new lines.

● **Give the Zoom command** (⌃Z).

As expected the printer options and the (RETURN) blobs are now hidden. This is how the file would look if it were printed. Now is a good time to save your work.

● **Give the Save command.**

Quick Check

4? Suppose you have a word processor file that contains no printer options. You insert a Centered printer option in the middle of the file. When the file is printed, what happens to the lines in the file before the printer option? What happens to the lines after the printer option?

- -

5? What printer option turns off centering?

- -

Justification Commands

In AppleWorks there are three formatting commands that control the position of text on a printed line. These are called **justification** commands. At each place in the file, only one justification command can be in effect. Figure 3-2 shows the effect of the three justification commands when text is printed.

Centered

```
                    A TALE OF TWO CITIES
                            by
                       Charles Dickens
```

Unjustified
(ragged right)

```
It was the best of times, it was the worst of times, it
was the age of wisdom, it was the age of foolishness,
It was the epoch of belief, it was the epoch of
incredulity, it was the season of Light, it was the
season of Darkness, it was the spring of hope, it was
the winter of despair, we had everything before us, we
had nothing before us.
```

Justified

```
It was the best of times, it was the worst of times, it
was the age of wisdom,  it was the age  of foolishness,
It was  the epoch of  belief,  it was  the  epoch of
incredulity,  it was  the season of Light,  it was  the
season of Darkness,  it was the spring of hope,  it was
the winter of despair,  we had everything before us, we
had nothing before us.
```

Justification styles. Three different ways to place printed text between the margins.

◆ **Centered lines**   When you insert the `Centered` printer option in a file, the computer begins putting spaces at the beginning of each line so that the text is centered between the left and right margins. The computer keeps centering lines until it reaches another justification command.

◆ **Unjustified lines**   When you insert the `Unjustified` printer option in a file, the computer starts printing lines at the left margin and prints as many words as possible without running past the right margin. Since the resulting lines will usually be of different lengths, this justification mode is sometimes called **ragged right**. If you insert no justification command in a file, the computer assumes you want unjustified lines.

◆ **Justified lines**   When you insert the `Justified` printer option in a file, the computer begins justifying text lines. That is, it inserts spaces between words as needed to make the first word begin at the left margin and the last word end at the right margin. Most books have justified lines. The effect is pleasing when the characters have different widths, but if the characters all have the same width, as is the case for most computer printers, the unjustified (ragged right) mode usually looks better.

◆ **Screen appearance**   All three justification commands affect the way lines appear when they are printed, but only two of them affect the way lines appear on the screen. Centered lines appear centered on the screen; unjustified lines appear unjustified on the screen; but justified lines do not appear justified on the screen. The extra spaces between words are added during printing.

Printing the File

You won't be adding any more printer options to file Tale in this lab. You just saved the file on your Data disk. You are now ready to print the file and see the effects of all the printer options. If there is a printer attached to your computer, you can print your file right now. If not you will have to take your Data disk to another computer that has a printer attached.

● **Follow the steps given on pages 50–51 to make a printed copy of file Tale. (If there is not enough time to print all pages, use ⒺⓈⒸ to stop printing as soon as page 2 begins.)**

● **Check the printed copy for the following things:**

   ▲ **The top, bottom, left, and right margins should be 1 inch.**

   ▲ **The first three text lines should be centered.**

If the margins on your printed copy are not 1 inch, the position of the paper in the printer probably needs to be adjusted.

This ends the regular activities in this lab. If you have time, do some of the On Your Own activities. When you have finished, quit AppleWorks.

On Your Own

■ Load file Poem into memory. Insert printer options so that the lines in the poem are centered. Set the top margin to 3 inches. Change the name of the file to Poem2 and save it on your Data disk. If a printer is available, use the steps on pages 50–51 to make a printed copy of the poem.

■ Create a word processor file from scratch. Name it Party. Write an invitation to a party. Use printer options to set the margins, and center any lines you like. Save the file on your Data disk. If a printer is available, make a printed copy of the invitation.

Review Questions

1. In AppleWorks what left and right margins are assumed if you do not tell the computer otherwise?

---

2. In AppleWorks what top and bottom margins are assumed if you do not tell the computer otherwise?

---

3. If you want the same margins to be used for the entire word processor file when it is printed, where should the margin printer options be placed in the file?

---

4. Suppose you want one paragraph in the middle of a word processor file to have wider left and right margins than the rest of the paragraphs. How would you do this?

---

5. Suppose a word processor file contains the printer option `Left Margin: 1.0 inches`. You want to change the left margin to 2 inches. How would you do this?

---

6. Suppose a word processor file contains no printer options. Then you insert the `Centered` printer option just ahead of a line in the middle of the file. What lines will be affected by this command?

---

7. What is the difference between a justified and an unjustified text line?

---

8. What does the term *ragged right* mean?

Goals

✔ Use printer options for single-, double-, and triple-spacing of lines.
✔ Use printer options to boldface and underline text.
✔ Use printer options to create headers and footers.

Controlling Line Spacing

So far in this chapter, you have learned how to tell the computer what size paper your printer uses, what margins you want, and how to center text between the margins. You can also tell the computer what spacing you want to have between printed lines. Let's look at that next.

Follow the Steps

● **Start the computer with AppleWorks.**

● **Load file Dickens from your Data disk.**

You will be making changes in this file and saving the new version on your disk. Now is a good time to change the file name.

● **Give the Name command ⌐N. Use the Yank command ⌐Y to erase the current name. Type** Tale2 **and tap** RETURN.

● **With the cursor at the beginning of the file, use the Option command ⌐O to set the paper width to 8.5 inches.**

● **Set the top and bottom margins to 1 inch.**

● **Return to the Review/Add/Change screen and give the Zoom command ⌐Z.**

You should see the three printer options you just inserted. They should be at the beginning of the file.

```
File: Tale2                    REVIEW/ADD/CHANGE          Escape: Main Menu
=====|====|====|====|====|====|====|====|====|====|====|====|====|====|====|===
--------Platen Width: 8.5 inches
--------Top Margin: 1.0 inches
--------Bottom Margin: 1.0 inches
※
—                      A TALE OF TWO CITIES※
※
```

● **Use the Calculate command ⌐K to see the page breaks. Then go to the end of the file.**

The text will fit on two pages. If you printed file Tale2 now, the text of each paragraph would be **single-spaced**. This means that there would be no blank lines between text lines. Sometimes you may want to have **double-spaced** or **triple-spaced** text. The extra blank lines allow room for handwritten comments or corrections on the printed copy. Changing the line spacing is easy to do in AppleWorks.

● **Put the cursor at the beginning of the first paragraph in the file.**

● **Give the Option command. Read the abbreviation at the right end of the highlighted line.**

The line-spacing options are listed near the end of the second column. As you can see, SS stands for Single Space. The other line-spacing options are DS for Double Space and TS for Triple Space.

● **Type DS and tap RETURN. Tap ESC to return to the Review/Add/Change screen.**

Notice that the Double Space printer option appears at the right place in the file, but the text lines following it still appear single-spaced. The line-spacing options do not affect the appearance of lines on the screen. The spacing shows up only when the file is printed. However, you can see one effect of changing the line spacing.

● **Give the Calculate command. Go to the end of the file.**

With the new double-spacing, it takes four pages to print the file. Before it took just two pages.

● **Go to the Printer Options screen. In the second column locate the option abbreviated LI.**

The Lines per Inch option is an interesting one. Most computers print six lines per inch down the page. Some printers can print lines closer together or farther apart than this. For example, many printers can print eight lines per inch. If your printer is one of these, you could insert the option Lines per inch: 8 to tell the computer to adjust the printer to this spacing. If you omit this option from a file, the computer assumes that six lines per inch will be printed.

● **Return to the Review/Add/Change screen.**

Quick Check

1? Suppose you insert a `Triple Space` printer option at the beginning of a file. What effect does this have on the appearance of the file on the Review/Add/Change screen?

2? Suppose you insert a `Triple Space` printer option at the beginning of a file. What effect does this have on the appearance of the file when it is printed?

3? Suppose you see printer options in a word processor file on the Review/Add/Change screen. How can you hide the printer options?

Boldfacing and Underlining

◆
★

Sometimes you may want to emphasize words or phrases when a file is printed. AppleWorks allows you to **underline** text, or to print the text in **boldface**.

Follow the Steps

● **Move the cursor to the beginning of the first paragraph in the file.**

The paragraph begins "It was the best of times, it was the worst of times." Suppose you want to emphasize "best" and "worst" by underlining the words. Here is how to do that.

● **Move the cursor under the** b **in** best. **Give the Option command.**

In the right column, you can see the printer options for `Underline Begin` and `Underline End`.

● **Type** UB **and tap** (RETURN). **Go back to the Review/Add/Change screen.**

Just left of the cursor, you should see a caret symbol (^). This symbol tells the computer where to begin underlining.

● **Move the cursor to the space after the word** best. **Give the Option command.**

● **Type** UE **and tap** (RETURN). **Go back to the Review/Add/Change screen.**

Now the word best is bracketed by caret symbols. The caret symbol has different meanings at different times. You can find what each symbol means by moving the cursor under the caret and reading the message at the bottom of the screen.

● **Move the cursor to the caret before the word** best. **Read the message at the bottom of the screen.**

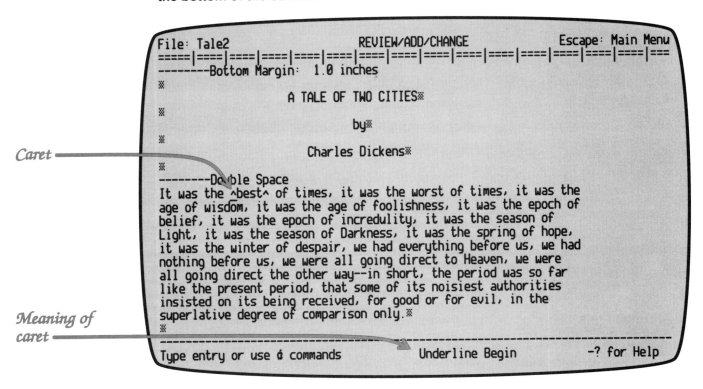

Caret

Meaning of caret

```
File: Tale2                    REVIEW/ADD/CHANGE            Escape: Main Menu
=====|====|====|====|====|====|====|====|====|====|====|====|====|====|====|===
---------Bottom Margin: 1.0 inches
  ※
                        A TALE OF TWO CITIES※

  ※                           by※

  ※                      Charles Dickens※

  ※
---------Double Space
It was the ^best^ of times, it was the worst of times, it was the
age of wisdom, it was the age of foolishness, it was the epoch of
belief, it was the epoch of incredulity, it was the season of
Light, it was the season of Darkness, it was the spring of hope,
it was the winter of despair, we had everything before us, we had
nothing before us, we were all going direct to Heaven, we were
all going direct the other way--in short, the period was so far
like the present period, that some of its noisiest authorities
insisted on its being received, for good or for evil, in the
superlative degree of comparison only.※
  ※
-------------------------------------------------------------------------------
Type entry or use ȯ commands          Underline Begin          -? for Help
```

This message confirms that the first caret tells the computer to begin underlining.

● **Move the cursor to the second caret.**

The second caret tells the computer to stop underlining. Now underline the word worst in the same sentence. This time use a shortcut.

● **Move the cursor under the** w **in** worst. **Type** (CONTROL L). ((CONTROL) **is at the left edge of the keyboard.)**

This caused the caret to be inserted without having to go to the Printer Option menu.

● **Move the cursor to the space after** worst. **Type** (CONTROL L) **again.**

Now the caret to turn off underlining is in place in the file.

● **Move the cursor under each new caret and read the message at the bottom of the screen.**

As you can see, the shortcut works. You can begin and end underlining either by giving the Option command or by typing (CONTROL L). A similar shortcut is available for beginning and ending boldface.

● **Move the cursor to the first character in** A TALE OF TWO CITIES. **Type** (CONTROL B).

● **Move the cursor just beyond the title. Type** (CONTROL B) **again.**

The title is now bracketed between caret symbols. (You could also insert these carets by giving the Option command and typing BB to begin boldface, BE to end it.)

● **Move the cursor under each of the new carets and read the message at the bottom of the screen.**

As you see, the new carets mark the beginning and end of boldface characters. We pointed out earlier that a caret can mean many different things. The only way to know what a caret means is to place the cursor under the caret and read the message at the bottom of the screen.

● **Use the Save command** (Ć S) **to put a copy of file Tale2 on your Data disk.**

Quick Check

4?   What is the quickest way to tell the computer to underline the word *wisdom*?

5?   Suppose you see a caret in an AppleWorks word processor file. How can you find out what the caret means?

Type Styles

Read This

As you have seen, you can emphasize a phrase by underlining it or printing it in boldface type. AppleWorks has formatting commands to control these and other **type styles**. Now is a good time to review the type styles you explored and learn about some new ones.

◆ **Boldface text**   There are two ways to mark a phrase for printing in boldface. One way is to place the cursor at the beginning of the phrase, go to the Printer Options screen, enter the Boldface Begin option, and return to the Review/Add/Change screen. Then move the cursor just beyond the end of the phrase and repeat the process, this time using the Boldface End option. Fortunately, as you have seen, there is a shortcut. After placing the cursor at the beginning of the phrase, type (CONTROL B). Move the cursor just beyond the end of the phrase and type (CONTROL B) again. You do not have to leave the Review/Add/Change screen if you use this shortcut.

◆ **Underlined text**   The steps for underlining a phrase are almost the same as the ones for printing a phrase in boldface type. The difference is that you use the `Underline Begin` and `Underline End` options on the Printer Options screen. There is also a shortcut for underlining: Type CONTROL-L at the beginning of the phrase and another CONTROL-L just past the end.

◆ **Superscripts and subscripts**   A superscript is text printed slightly above the rest of the text on the line. A subscript is text printed slightly below the line. AppleWorks has printer options that allow you to mark text to be printed as either a superscript or a subscript. The printer options `Superscript Beg` and `Superscript End` are used to mark the beginning and end of superscript text. `Subscript Begin` and `Subscript End` are used for subscripts. There is no shortcut for these printer options.

```
This is the regular type
style. ^Now we shift into
boldface.^ The word
^important^ is underlined.

The 2 in the formula H^2^0
is a subscript.

The 2s in r^2^ = x^2^ + y^2^
are examples of superscripts.
```

This is the regular type style. **Now we shift into boldface**. The word <u>important</u> is underlined.

The 2 in the formula H_2O is a subscript.

The 2s in $r^2 = x^2 + y^2$ are examples of superscripts.

The four type styles available in AppleWorks. The left frame shows type style carets on the screen. The right frame shows printed results.

◆ **Appearance on screen**   Type style printer options look different on the screen from the other options you have used. When you insert any of the eight type style printer options, the computer displays a caret (^) at the cursor position. Later, when you read the text on the screen and see a caret, you may have forgotten what it means. Is it just a caret in the text? Is it a type style option? If so which type style option is it?

◆ **Checking the caret**   AppleWorks provides an easy answer to these questions. Move the cursor to a caret in the text. If the caret stands for a type style printer option, the name of the option will appear at the bottom of the screen. Otherwise you will see the usual line and column numbers there.

◆ **Deleting type style options**   You can remove type style options from the file the same way that you remove ordinary text. One way is to put the cursor just to the right of the caret and tap DELETE. Another way is to put the cursor on the caret, give the Delete command (⌘D), and tap RETURN. Either way the caret disappears from the file and so does the printer option.

◆ **Printer limitations**   AppleWorks allows you to mark text to be printed in four special type styles: boldface, underline, superscript, and subscript. Not all printers can create text in all these styles, however. As with other format commands, your printer places limits on what you can do.

Adding Page Headers and Footers

When you print a long file, it is useful to have the computer print page numbers at the top or bottom of each page. You may also want other information printed on each page. To do this, you must use a format command to define a one-line **header** or **footer**.

Follow the Steps

● **File Tale2 should be visible on the Review/Add/Change screen.**

Here is how the beginning of the file should look:

```
File: Tale2                  REVIEW/ADD/CHANGE          Escape: Main Menu
====|====|====|====|====|====|====|====|====|====|====|====|====|===
--------Platen Width:  8.5 inches
--------Top Margin:  1.0 inches
--------Bottom Margin:  1.0 inches
⌘
                    ^A TALE OF TWO CITIES^⌘
⌘
                            by⌘
⌘
                       Charles Dickens⌘
⌘
--------Double Space
It was the ^best^ of times, it was the ^worst^ of times, it was
the age of wisdom, it was the age of foolishness, it was the
```

There should be three printer options at the top and one just before the first paragraph. There should be carets around the title and the words best and worst. Here's how to add a footer to each page.

● **Move the cursor just below the three printer options at the top of the screen. Give the Options command.**

In the third column you will find the Page Header and Page Footer abbreviations. You want to create a footer.

● **Type FO and tap (RETURN). Go back to the Review/Add/Change screen.**

You have inserted a Page Footer option. The next step is to enter the text that you want to appear in the footer line. The cursor is properly positioned for you to do this.

● **Type the line below. Tap (RETURN) when the line is correct.**

A Tale of Two Cities -- Page

When the computer finds a Page Footer option in a file, it uses the next line of text as the footer. So the line you just typed will appear at the bottom of each page. Now tell the computer to print the page number right after Page in your footer.

● **Move the cursor just after Page.**

● **Type a space. Then give the Options command.**

● **Find the abbreviation for the** Print Page No. **option. (Do *not* use the** Page Number **option.)**

● **Type the abbreviation and tap** (RETURN).

This inserts a caret just after the space you typed in the footer.

● **Return to the Review/Add/Change screen. Move the cursor under the new caret. Read the message at the bottom of the screen.**

This time the caret tells the computer to print the current page number at the position of the caret.

Footer text —

Caret —

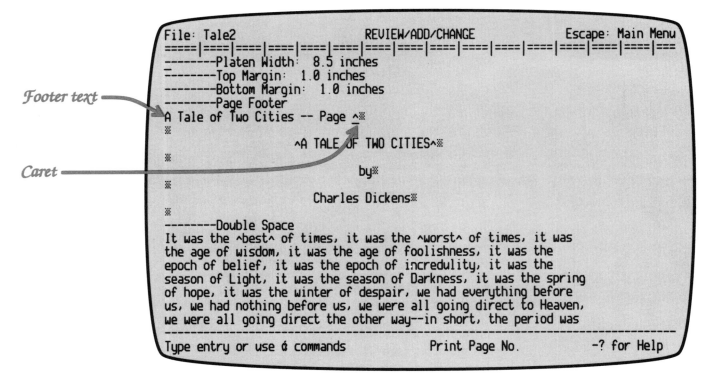

```
File: Tale2                    REVIEW/ADD/CHANGE            Escape: Main Menu
=====|====|====|====|====|====|====|====|====|====|====|====|====|====|===
--------Platen Width:  8.5 inches
--------Top Margin:  1.0 inches
--------Bottom Margin:  1.0 inches
--------Page Footer
A Tale of Two Cities -- Page ^▒
 ▒
                        ^A TALE OF TWO CITIES^▒
 ▒
                                 by▒
 ▒
                           Charles Dickens▒
 ▒
--------Double Space
It was the ^best^ of times, it was the ^worst^ of times, it was
the age of wisdom, it was the age of foolishness, it was the
epoch of belief, it was the epoch of incredulity, it was the
season of Light, it was the season of Darkness, it was the spring
of hope, it was the winter of despair, we had everything before
us, we had nothing before us, we were all going direct to Heaven,
we were all going direct the other way--in short, the period was
--------------------------------------------------------------------------
Type entry or use ô commands            Print Page No.          -? for Help
```

So far, so good: You have created a footer line that will print the title and page number on each page. As it stands, the footer will appear at the left margin. You would probably prefer to see it centered. You already know how to center text.

● **Move the cursor to the beginning of the footer line. Use the Options command to insert a** Centered **printer option.**

Now the footer line is centered, but so are all the other lines in the file. You must turn centering off after the footer line.

● **Go back to the Review/Add/Change screen. Place the cursor just below the footer line.**

● **Use the Options command to insert an** Unjustified **printer option.**

That completes your definition of the footer. As stated earlier the computer will now print two blank lines and the footer line just above the bottom margin on each page. These three extra lines will take up ½ inch in addition to your 1-inch margin. To balance things, decrease the bottom margin to ½ inch.

● **Use the Delete command to remove the present** Bottom Margin **printer option from the file.**

● **Insert a new** Bottom Margin **option. Make the margin 0.5 inches wide.**

● **Go back to the Review/Add/Change screen.**

The printer options are now all correct, and the file is ready to be printed. Here is how your screen should look now:

```
File: Tale2                 REVIEW/ADD/CHANGE           Escape: Main Menu
=====|====|====|====|====|====|====|====|====|====|====|====|====|====|===
--------Platen Width:  8.5 inches
--------Top Margin:  1.0 inches
--------Bottom Margin:  0.5 inches
=-------Page Footer
--------Centered
                   A Tale of Two Cities -- Page ^▒
--------Unjustified
 ▒
                      ^A TALE OF TWO CITIES^▒

 ▒
                              by▒

 ▒
                        Charles Dickens▒

 ▒
--------Double Space
It was the ^best^ of times, it was the ^worst^ of times, it was
the age of wisdom, it was the age of foolishness, it was the
epoch of belief, it was the epoch of incredulity, it was the
season of Light, it was the season of Darkness, it was the spring
of hope, it was the winter of despair, we had everything before
------------------------------------------------------------------------
Type entry or use ₲ commands          Line 4  Column 1        -? for Help
```

● **Give the Zoom command to hide the printer options.**

The computer hides all your options but one—the Page Footer option. The reason for this is to make clear that one of the lines in the file is a footer and not part of the regular text.

6? Suppose a file contains a `Page Footer` option. Which line of the file contains the text of the footer?

7? How do you tell the computer to insert the current page number after the word `page` in a word processor file?

Printing the File

◆
★

You won't be adding any more printer options to your file. Now is a good time to save your work.

Follow the Steps

● **Use the Save command to move a copy of file Tale2 to your Data disk.**

You are now ready to print the file and see the effects of all the printer options. If there is a printer attached to your computer, you can print your file right now. If not you will have to take your Data disk to another computer that has a printer attached.

● **Follow the steps given on pages 50–51 to make a printed copy of file Tale2. (If there is not enough time to print all four pages, use ⒺⓈⒸ to stop printing as soon as page 2 begins.)**

● **Check the printed copy for the following things:**

  ▲ **The title should be printed in boldface type.**

  ▲ **The words** best **and** worst **in the first paragraph should be underlined.**

  ▲ **The lines in each paragraph should be double-spaced.**

  ▲ **The top, left, and right margins should be 1 inch wide.**

  ▲ **There should be a centered footer on each page. The footer should contain the proper page number.**

  ▲ **The bottom margin should be ½ inch below the footer.**

More About Headers and Footers

◆
★

In your lab work you have seen how to put footers into a word processor file and to have the page number printed as part of the footer. The same method can be used to have headers printed on each page. Now is a good time to review this topic.

♦ **Footer and header location**   The figure below shows the layout used by AppleWorks for headers and footers. The header appears below the top margin. The header consists of one line of text followed by two blank lines. The footer appears above the bottom margin and consists of two blank lines followed by one line of text. The header and the footer each take up three lines on the page. The body of the text falls below the header and above the footer.

Top margin	
Header	A Tale of Two Cities
Body	likely enough that in the rough outhouses of some tillers of the heavy lands adjacent to Paris, there were sheltered from the weather that very day, rude carts, bespattered with rustic mire, snuffed about by pigs, and roosted in by poultry, which the Farmer, Death, had already set apart to be his tumbrils of the Revolution. But that Woodman and that Farmer, though they work unceasingly, work silently, and no one heard them as they went about with muffled tread: the rather, forasmuch as to entertain any suspicion that they were awake, was to be atheistical and traitorous. In England, there was scarcely an amount of order and protection to justify much national boasting. Daring burglaries by armed men, and highway
Footer	
	page 3
Bottom margin	

Location of Apple-Works headers and footers. The top margin is above the header and the bottom margin is below the footer.

♦ **Creating a header**   Suppose you want to create a header that will appear on every page of a document. The first step is to put the cursor before the first line of text. Next give the Options command and choose `Page Header`. Then return to the Review/Add/Change screen. The computer inserts the `Page Header` option into the file. The line of text just below this option will be the header. Therefore the final step is to insert the line that you want printed as the header.

♦ **Creating a footer**   The steps for creating a footer are the same as for creating a header. The only difference is that you choose the `Page Footer` option. The text line following the `Page Footer` option in the text will be printed at the bottom of each page.

♦ **Formatting headers and footers**   Suppose you want a header to have left and right margins different from the rest of the text, or to be centered, or to have any other special formatting. To do this you must insert the necessary formatting commands before the header text line. Remember, however, that these formatting commands will apply not just to the header line but to the rest of the text in the file. So you should undo any special printer options that you want to apply only to the header. For example, if you use a `Centered` option before the header, you should insert an `Unjustified` or `Justified` option right after the header text line. You can do special formatting of footers the same way.

◆ **Changing headers and footers**   Sometimes you want a header or a footer to remain the same throughout a document. At other times, you may want to change headers or footers at different places in the document. This is easy to do in AppleWorks. Simply insert a new `Page Header` or `Page Footer` option and the new text line into the file wherever you want the change to occur. The change takes effect the next time the header or footer is to be printed.

◆ **Page numbers**   One important use of headers or footers is to print the current page number on each page. AppleWorks has a formatting command that tells the computer to print the current page number whenever this command appears. This command, `Print Page No.`, can be inserted into any text line but is usually used in header and footer lines. As with the type style printer options, the computer displays a caret where this option is inserted.

This ends the regular activities in the lab. If you have time, do some of the On Your Own activities below. Then quit AppleWorks.

On Your Own

■ Adding a header is just like adding a footer. Move the cursor just below the printer options now at the beginning of file Tale2. Insert a header that contains your name and today's date. Print the file. Now move the `Page Header` printer option and the header line so that they appear just after the title. Print the file again. What is different this time?

■ In file Tale2, change the `Unjustified` printer option to `Justified`. Print the file and look for differences. Insert a `New Page` printer option just after the line `Charles Dickens`. Print the file and see what happens.

Review Questions

1. Suppose you want an entire document to be double-spaced when it is printed. How would you do this? How would you then tell the computer to single-space one paragraph in the middle of the document?

- -

2. Suppose you insert the printer option `Lines per Inch` and at the prompt enter 8. What does this tell the computer to do? Will this always work?

- -

3. What type styles are available in AppleWorks?

    _____

4. What are two different ways to mark the beginning of a phrase to be underlined
    when printed?

    _____

5. How can you identify type style printer options on the screen?

    _____

6. Suppose you have identified a type style printer option on the screen. How can
    you tell which one it is?

    _____

7. What is a subscript? What is a superscript?

    _____

8. How can you delete a type style printer option from an AppleWorks word
    processor file?

    _____

9. What is a header? What is a footer?

    _____

10. In AppleWorks what text line does the computer use as a header?

    _____

11. Suppose you want the left and right margins for a header to be ½ inch; you also
    want the left and right margins for the rest of the document to be 1 inch. How
    would you do this?

    _____

12. Once you define a header, how long does it remain in effect?

    _____

13. How would you tell the computer to print the current page number as part of
    the text of a footer?

    _____

Goals

✔ Adjust paper size and margins for the word processor project.
✔ Design a cover page for the project.
✔ Adjust line spacing and select font styles.
✔ Add a footer containing the page number.
✔ Print the file.

Making Final Changes

Follow the Steps

In Chapter 2 you planned and wrote a paper, which you saved in file MyPaper. In this lab you will put formatting commands in the file and print it.

● **Start the computer with AppleWorks. Load file MyPaper from your Data disk.**

This is a good time to have one final look at your paper before preparing it for the printer.

● **Read the paper and make any last-minute changes.**

The material at the beginning of the file was useful while you were planning and writing the paper. This material is no longer needed. Get rid of it before thinking about formatting commands.

● **Move the cursor to the top of the file. Give the Delete command ⌐Ⓓ.**

● **Use cursor commands to highlight all the planning material above your paper. Then tap ⟨RETURN⟩.**

Now the file should contain only your actual paper. (If you deleted too much, remove the file from the Desktop, throw away changes, and load a new copy from your Data disk.)

Paper Size and Margins

Now it is time to plan the way you want the paper to look when it is printed. To set the paper size and margins, you will use the printer options you learned about earlier. First make certain that the printer options will be visible when you insert them.

Follow the Steps

- **Give the Zoom command ⓐⓏ.**

  There should be no printer options in the file now. You should, however, see the blobs showing where ⟨RETURN⟩ was tapped.

- **Move the cursor to the top of the file. Give the Options command ⓐⓄ.**

  Recall that the Platen Width and Paper Length printer options tell the computer what size paper is in the printer.

- **In the highlighted line see what values are set for the size of the paper.**

- **If necessary change the values to match the paper you will be using.**

  That takes care of the paper size. Next decide on the top, bottom, left, and right margins.

- **See what values are set for the margins. If you wish, change the values to ones you want.**

- **Go back to the Review/Add/Change screen.**

  If you changed the paper size or margins, you should see the new printer options at the beginning of the file. (If you entered an incorrect printer option, you must use the Delete command to erase it and then enter the correct option.)

A Cover Page

Many people like to have a cover page on papers they write. This page shows the title of the paper, who wrote it, the date, and any other important information.

Follow the Steps

- **Move the cursor to the first line of text in your paper.**

- **On separate lines, with blank lines between, enter the title of your paper, your name, and the date.**

  The text for your cover page is now in the file. Now you need to tell the computer to begin a new page after the cover page is printed.

● **If necessary move the cursor just below the last line to go on the cover page.**

● **Give the Options command. Enter the printer option** `New Page`.

The `New Page` printer option should appear between the last line of the cover page and the first line of your paper. Now decide how the cover page should look. First it is usual to put some blank lines above the title of the paper.

● **Go back to the Review/Add/Change screen. Put the cursor at the beginning of the line containing the title.**

● **Give the Options command. Set the** `Skip Lines` **option to** `15`.

This will make the title appear 15 lines below the top margin when the cover page is printed. Next center all text lines on the cover page. The cursor is already at the right place to do this.

● **Enter the** `Centered` **printer option. Go back to the Review/Add/Change screen.**

The new printer option should appear just below the `Skip Lines...` option. Remember that you must also tell the computer where to stop centering lines.

● **Move the cursor just below the last line to go on the title page.**

● **Give the Options command. Enter the** `Unjustified` **printer option. Go back to the Review/Add/Change screen.**

Now only the lines on the cover page will be centered. If you want other information to appear on the cover page, enter it now and add any necessary printer options.

Line Spacing, Fonts, and a Footer

Your new cover page is now complete. Now it's time to turn to the paper itself. You have learned how to change line spacing and have words underlined or printed in boldface.

● **Move the cursor to the first line after the** `New Page` **printer option. Give the Options command.**

The highlighted line shows that the `Single Space` option is in effect now.

● **If you want** `Double Space` **or** `Triple Space` **options, enter your choice now.**

You may wish some words in your paper to appear underlined or in boldface. To accomplish this you must move the cursor to the beginning of the text, type (CONTROL)(L) or (CONTROL)(B), and do the same thing at the character after the end of the text.

● **Find and mark any words you want to appear underlined or in boldface.**

As a final step before printing, add a footer that will print the page number at the bottom of each page after the cover page.

● **Move the cursor to the first line after the** New Page **printer option. Give the Options command. Then enter the options and text below:**

```
--------Page Footer
--------Centered
Word Processor Project -- Page ^
--------UnJustified
```

The caret after Page comes from using the Print Page No. printer option.

● **Use the Save command (d)(S) to put a copy of the new version of file MyPaper on your Data disk.**

Printing the File

All the writing and formatting are now complete. At last it is time to print your paper. If no printer is connected to your computer, you must take your disk to another computer with a printer.

Follow the Steps

● **Follow the steps on pages 50–51 to make a printed copy of file MyPaper.**

When you see the printed copy of your paper, you may discover errors or decide on different printer options.

● **Make any changes you wish. Save the new version. Print it again.**

This completes your word processor project. In it you have used all the important AppleWorks tools for writing, editing, and formatting. There are many such tools, and you may have had trouble remembering them. After a little practice, however, they will become second nature and will make most writing tasks much easier.

● **When you have finished, quit AppleWorks in the usual way.**

Keyboard Commands

⌘K, **Calculate**	Find and display all page breaks in a word processor file.
⌘O, **Printer Options**	Display a list of word processor format commands.
⌘Z, **Zoom**	Display or hide format commands and (RETURN) blobs in a word processor file.

Format Comands

Boldface Begin	Begin printing characters in boldface type.
Boldface End	Stop printing characters in boldface type.
Bottom Margin	Set the bottom margin on following pages to the number of inches given.
Centered	Begin centering lines between the left and right margins.
Double Space	Begin printing a blank line after each text line.
Justified	Begin printing lines at the left margin and adding spaces between words so that lines end at the right margin.
Left Margin	Set the left margin on following pages to the number of inches given.
Lines per Inch	Set the number of lines per inch to be used by the printer.
New Page	Begin a new page.
Page Footer	Begin printing the next text line in the file (preceded by two blank lines) just above the bottom margin on each page.
Page Header	Begin printing the next text line in the file (followed by two blank lines) just below the top margin on each page.
Paper Length	Tell the computer how many inches long the paper in your printer is.
Platen Width	Tell the computer how many inches wide the paper in your printer is.
Print Page Number	Print the current page number at this point in the text.

Right Margin	Set the right margin on following pages to the number of inches given.
Single Space	Begin printing lines with no extra blank lines between them.
Skip Lines	Space down the number of lines given.
Subscript Begin	Begin printing characters below the normal position.
Subscript End	Stop printing characters below the normal position.
Superscript Begin	Begin printing characters above the normal position.
Superscript End	Stop printing characters above the normal position.
Top Margin	Set the top margin on following pages to the number of inches given.
Triple Space	Begin printing two blank lines after each text line.
Underline Begin	Begin underlining characters.
Underline End	Stop underlining characters.
Unjustified	Begin printing lines at the left margin.

New Ideas

boldface text	A type style in which characters are darker than usual.
double-spaced text	Text printed with a blank line after each text line.
footer	Text that is repeated at the bottom of each page.
format	The appearance of a word processor file when it is printed. Format is determined by the page layout and type styles used.
format command	A word processor command that affects the format of a printed document.
header	Text that is repeated at the top of each page.
justify	Add space between words to make a group of printed lines have the same length.
line length	The distance in inches between the left and right margins. In other words, it is the page width minus the width of the two margins.
margin	White space at one of the four edges of a printed page.
page layout	Physical location of printed text on the page. This is controlled mainly by the margins, paper size, headers, footers, figures, and number of columns.
printer option	The AppleWorks term for a format command.
ragged right	Text printed so that each line begins at the left margin but is not justified.

single-spaced text   Text printed without extra blank lines after each text line.

triple-spaced text   Text printed with two blank lines after each text line.

type style   The size, shape, or other special feature used to print each character in a word processor file.

underlined text   A type style in which each character has a horizontal line printed beneath it.

WYSIWYG   Abbreviation for "What you see is what you get." A WYSIWYG word processor program attempts to display on the screen exactly what a file will look like when it is printed.